Small Unit Leadership
Training for new to mid-level leadership

The Ballard Rules
Second Edition with Post-Mayoral Comments

Greg Ballard
MAYOR, INDIANAPOLIS 2008-2015
LT. COL., U.S. MARINES (RET) • CORPORATE MANAGER

authorHOUSE®

AuthorHouse™
1663 Liberty Drive
Bloomington, IN 47403
www.authorhouse.com
Phone: 1 (800) 839-8640

© 2005, 2016 Greg Ballard. All rights reserved.

No part of this book may be reproduced, stored in a retrieval system, or transmitted by any means without the written permission of the author.

Cover photo by Rob Banayote.

Published by AuthorHouse 11/04/2016

ISBN: 978-1-5246-2075-2 (sc)
ISBN: 978-1-5246-2076-9 (e)

Library of Congress Control Number: 2005901105

Print information available on the last page.

Any people depicted in stock imagery provided by Thinkstock are models, and such images are being used for illustrative purposes only. Certain stock imagery © Thinkstock.

This book is printed on acid-free paper.

Because of the dynamic nature of the Internet, any web addresses or links contained in this book may have changed since publication and may no longer be valid. The views expressed in this work are solely those of the author and do not necessarily reflect the views of the publisher, and the publisher hereby disclaims any responsibility for them.

For my (now older) kids, Erica and Greg

CONTENTS

FOREWORD ix

ACKNOWLEDGMENTS xi

INTRODUCTION... xiii

Chapter 1	MY FIRST LIGHT BULB MOMENT 1
Chapter 2	WHAT IS LEADERSHIP AND WHY IS IT IMPORTANT?... 2
Chapter 3	TWO OVERARCHING RESPONSIBILITIES.................. 4
Chapter 4	INDICATORS OF EFFECTIVE LEADERSHIP 5
Chapter 5	LEADERSHIP REALITIES 7
Chapter 6	LEADERSHIP TRAITS 21
Chapter 7	LEADERSHIP PRINCIPLES 37
Chapter 8	IMPORTANT DEFINITIONS AND SOME SERIOUS LOGIC 51
Chapter 9	IF YOU HAVE HIRING AND FIRING AAUTHORITY 53
Chapter 10	OTHER THOUGHTS 55
Chapter 11	POST-MAYORAL COMMENTS 62
Appendix	A SUMMARY OF IMPORTANT POINTS 76
	RECOMMENDED READING 83

FOREWORD

In 2008, I met Greg Ballard a few weeks after he became the forty-eighth Mayor of Indianapolis. A small team of community leaders was traveling to Phoenix to observe the 2008 Super Bowl operation to determine if we would join a short list of other cities in the hypercompetitive race to host the 2012 Super Bowl.

My initial impression was that he was quiet and reserved, a stark contrast to the other highly charged and animated traveling team members. He was also remarkably unpretentious.

What I came to learn over the next four years as president and CEO of the Host Committee for Super Bowl XLVI was that these unusual qualities form a different kind of charisma and define Greg Ballard as an exceptional leader. His quiet strength, coupled with a humble demeanor and big heart, would allow him to preside over our city as it hosted one of the most acclaimed and organized Super Bowls of all time and to become one of the most accomplished and beloved mayors in a long line of remarkable Indianapolis leaders.

There are three things about this quiet, unassuming man that make him an uncommon and unique leader. First, and perhaps surprisingly for a senior elected official in a major US city, his compass was set on doing the right thing for the long term. He expected his team to excel at the day-to-day blocking and tackling of required duties to fulfill obligations, but his passion and key initiatives were molded by a long-term view rather than short-term political gain.

Putting politics second in a mayoral role often creates short-term criticism, which leads to a second fundamental strength of Greg Ballard—he is a rock in all circumstances, and he is unflappable. People around him knew that once a decision was made, he would not waiver, and there would be no second-guessing the course once it was set. This approach was refreshing, inspiring, and efficient.

Largely because of these two characteristics, his third great strength was his ability to attract remarkably talented and energetic people to his team. Exceptional people desire a leader who will guide, teach, trust, and support them, but not micromanage them. Greg's reputation in this critical area of successful leadership is like a magnet, and the talent pool around him speaks for itself.

These three essential Ballard characteristics are fundamentally how I see him. The specifics of this book offer more detailed insights into his effective leadership and how it can be replicated. While this book is a quick read, you are likely to find yourself going back to it time and time again to fully understand and apply the wisdom in The Ballard Rules. It was a blessing for me to work alongside Greg the last nine years from a close vantage point. He is the true definition of an exceptional leader in action.

—Allison Melangton

ACKNOWLEDGMENTS

My wife, Winnie, has been with me for over thirty years and it has been an extraordinary journey. We were married when I was a young Marine officer, and during my twenty-three years in the Corps, I served in war and in peace, and we lived around the world. Moving back to Indianapolis from Stuttgart, Germany and entering the private sector was stressful, but we managed. Deciding to run for Mayor was not something she had foreseen (neither had I), but she was right there with me. Now as we try to give back and set up for retirement (whatever that means), we still just enjoy each other's company. I've been blessed.

We would not be re-publishing this book without a successful two terms as Mayor of Indianapolis. Entering the political arena brings new relationships, most of which have been very positive. As I say in my Post-Mayoral comments inside, I had a tremendous staff all eight years as the Mayor. Recognizing them all would be a very long list indeed, so to thank my entire staff, I will mention my four Chiefs of Staff, all of whom seemed to have the right skill set for the city at the right time. Paul Okeson, Chris Cotterill, Ryan Vaughn, and Jason Dudich all spent enormous time and effort in bettering our city. The Chief of Staff position in my administration had tremendous responsibility and latitude, and all of them proved to be extremely competent and effective.

My beloved "political hacks" that I talk about inside also deserve mention. I still maintain contact with most of them, as they are still very helpful and of great value. I really came to appreciate their views and their concern. Two of them, Jennifer Hallowell and Robert Vane, remain good friends to this day and helped with the additional comments in this book. Kyle Walker has stood by me since early 2007. I would not have become Mayor without his help, and his behind-the-scenes support throughout the two terms contributed to our success. All three still look out for me and I can't thank them enough.

Officeholders rarely mention anything about lawyers publicly, but two of them, Bob Grand and Joe Loftus, were there at the very beginning when no one thought I would win in 2007. They were of great counsel to me before, during and now after my time as Mayor. I was a more effective Mayor because of them.

Lastly, two other people have come to mean a lot to Winnie and me. Melissa Proffitt Schmidt and Dave Sherman, both of whom we met as a result of my election, have become very good friends to us. They have helped us along in so many ways and made the life of an elected official and his wife much more pleasant and productive.

INTRODUCTION

A few years back, a pro football quarterback with tremendous physical gifts said that "Leadership is overrated." Importantly, he is a fine, decent man who anonymously helps out in his community, but professionally, he never came close to leading his team to the Super Bowl.

Leadership is underrated; it is certainly not overrated. Think of turnarounds in many different types of organizations and you can almost always attribute the turnaround, whether positive or negative, to a change of people in positions of leadership.

Leadership is a learned behavior. Some people pick up leadership skills as they grow up, but you can also learn leadership through study, practice, and reflective thought. Although I am introverted, I was able to hold some difficult leadership positions successfully. If leadership could not be learned, then the U.S. military could not have become the organization it is today. Every branch of service teaches leadership from day one and I can attest that young leaders in the military come from all types of backgrounds with all types of personalities. I have seen great leaders who were very outgoing and those who were quiet and reserved. Some strictly followed the rule book; others couldn't find the rule book and had no desire to do so. Some were extremely humble, some not so humble. However, there were similarities amongst them all in their personality traits, in the way they exercised leadership responsibilities, and in their understanding of the realities of leadership. I also observed these same characteristics in great leaders in the civilian world. These similarities are the focus of this book

<u>This book is designed to help those leaders who have people junior to them but also have senior leaders above them</u>. You will not find anecdotes in this book about presidents, CEO's, four-star generals or the like. *Great leadership routinely occurs at the "rubber meets the road" level.* I am not discounting higher level leadership; most of the people who get to the top of an organization have earned it. It just is not the focus of this book. Helping new, junior, and middle level leaders understand the requirements and the realities of leading is the focus of this book. I have seen far too many junior leaders who were placed in a position of responsibility and

did not have a clue as to how to successfully influence a group of people to get something done.

This book is a combination of philosophy and practicality. It is designed to give leaders, or potential leaders, insight into what leadership is; detail some realities of leadership that you will probably not find anywhere else; and then to discuss those traits and principles that I believe are endemic to leadership. It also gives you three very important indicators to determine if you are an effective leader.

I began studying leadership intently when I was the Commanding Officer of a Marine Corps Recruiting Station, filling a position equivalent to a civilian regional sales manager, covering the southern two-thirds of Illinois and the eastern third of Missouri. It was a job filled with enormous pressure. All of my Marines were used to a strong, visible command structure, but the geographical separation of the organization made force of personality much more important than otherwise would have been required with a more visible leadership support structure. Other than our monthly awards/training session, I frequently had only one face-to-face meeting per month with my junior leaders. I had to positively influence them in a very short period of time. It is what I called "raw, naked leadership." It was very difficult. I did it better than some, some did it better than I did. However, it did cause me to read about and study extensively all styles and facets of leadership in many different disciplines.

The realities, traits, principles, and the other thoughts contained in this book are culled from my years as a leader in the Marines, in the corporate world, in coaching, and as a small business owner. I also had some great mentors who provided me with terrific insight, and their wisdom is certainly incorporated in this book. The accumulated knowledge contained herein will apply whether you are leading a military unit, a sales team, warehouse workers, a group of scientists, basketball players, a non-profit, or any other type of organization.

I hope you enjoy reading this book as much as I enjoyed writing it.

Tips on reading this book

I use "he" and "she" interchangeably throughout. The old way of writing required the masculine to be used, but I decided that the world has changed since then.

I refer to "enterprise," "organization," and "department" throughout the book. Generally speaking, enterprise refers to a very large activity. Organization is a medium to big activity, such as a singly-focused company or division. Department usually refers to the activity that is under the charge of a junior to middle level leader.

"Employee" is used frequently for simplicity, but it could refer to teacher, team member, player, or the like.

Those sentences or phrases that are italicized are repeated in summary form in the appendix. They make for a good refresher on small unit leadership when desired.

Chapter 1

MY FIRST LIGHT BULB MOMENT

My first "light bulb moment" on leadership came while I was a lowly Marine officer candidate in Quantico, Virginia in 1978. Officer Candidate School (OCS) is a screening process to weed out those whose leadership potential is deemed wanting. Candidate responsibilities were rotated routinely so that candidates could be evaluated on their leadership abilities. I really had no idea what leadership was and frankly can't remember ever thinking about the concept until I reached Quantico.

I failed miserably in my first stab at leadership. The first few weeks of OCS, my focus was on taking care of myself by learning, being on time, and generally running through the paces of OCS. Then, a few weeks into the school, I was made a squad leader in the platoon. After attending a morning class, the platoon had the usual two minutes to unload our books, get our packs ready, and be in formation ready for a nice hike. I was determined to be one of the first candidates out in formation, and I was. There I was standing in the squad leader's position at the front of the largely empty column, when the Sergeant Instructor of our platoon put his face right up against mine and said as loudly and snidely as possible "Where's your squad?" Oh!

It was at that moment *I realized I was no longer being judged on how I performed, but on how those people assigned to me performed*. It was a scary thought.

Chapter 2

WHAT IS LEADERSHIP AND WHY IS IT IMPORTANT?

Despite the volumes written on leadership, I find very few definitions of the actual word. I define it as below:

<u>Leadership</u> - The ability to successfully influence a group of people to achieve a desired outcome.

It seems like a simple enough definition, but there are two key words in this definition, "influence" and "outcome."

<u>Influence</u> is the essence of what leaders do. They use their personalities, knowledge, actions, and understandings to motivate their employees to achieve the desired results. Leaders who achieve the best results are those who understand certain realities, possess a positive mix of character traits, and consistently execute reliable principles.

The desired <u>outcome</u> is why leaders are chosen for a particular position or responsibility. Results must be achieved. It may be a singular result, such as a game victory, or it may be a continuing series of results, such as in business where companies must show profit on a continuing basis.

Leadership is important because people naturally look for direction to achieve outcomes. In any structured organization, there is always someone in charge. So-called co-equal teams solving a problem have to report to a boss who will make the ultimate decision either by approving or overturning the solution achieved by the co-equals. Even in the absence of a formal structure, a leader will emerge. He may be a good or a bad leader, but he will emerge.

There is a truth that I have discovered throughout my years of leading people and observing other leaders. You must believe this to be an effective leader:

If <u>most</u> of your employees are acting one way, either well or poorly, it is a <u>direct</u> result of your leadership.

What is Leadership and Why is It Important?

The majority of people in any group want to do a good job. *If things are not going well, there is still leadership in your department. Either you are a bad leader or someone else is filling the leadership role in a negative manner.* Look in the mirror for the problem and the solution. Always remember, <u>people want to succeed and they want the designated leader to take them to that success.</u>

Chapter 3

TWO OVERARCHING RESPONSIBILITIES

In any organization, there are always two overarching responsibilities incumbent upon leaders. They are:

- To achieve the desired outcome

- To look out for the welfare of their people

Leaders are placed in positions of responsibility to get the job done. They are expected to use their skills and knowledge to properly influence people under their charge. Whether the desired outcome is a one-time result or an ongoing series of results, leaders are first required to get the job done. Using guidance from your senior leaders, <u>you must clearly understand what is required</u> and then set about getting it accomplished.

Leaders must look out for the welfare of their people for two reasons. First, it is required because it is a moral norm in our society. Second, if leaders do not look out for their people's welfare in current situations, there will be very few, if any, people who will want them as leaders in the future. It is difficult to be a good leader if no one wants to follow you.

The context of taking care of your people is situational dependent. I remember a former Commandant of the Marine Corps telling a class I was attending that, in wartime, welfare of the troops was coming home alive, but not at the expense of failing to accomplish the mission. That is not quite the same as giving extra time off or fighting for safer working conditions.

Whatever the context, taking care of your people will, over time, enable you to achieve your goals more readily. *These two overarching responsibilities always work together.*

Chapter 4

INDICATORS OF EFFECTIVE LEADERSHIP

How do you know if an organization is being effectively led? There are three key indicators you can use to determine if the leadership of an organization is effective. *All three must be present to indicate truly effective leadership.* They are:

- **Proficiency** – The organization knows the job thoroughly and does it well

- **Organizational Discipline** – In the absence of the leader or key personnel, the organization executes well and initiates appropriate action

- **High Morale** – Employees exhibit a positive state of mind; they are proud to be part of the organization

Proficiency is a result of both individual and group training. Despite past credentials, *no individual is properly trained until his actions contribute positively to the group.* Never assume proficiency. Train if necessary, then inspect for proficiency.

Organizational discipline can only occur if the leader has clearly set proper standards and expectations. The setting of standards and the expectations surrounding those standards allows a well-trained organization to function effectively during an occasional absence by the leader.

High morale indicates that proficiency and organizational discipline are well received, indeed, expected by the people in the organization. Organizations can have proficiency and discipline without high morale, but the proficiency and discipline will come from fear or another negative leadership trait. Experience tells me that negative leadership works for only short periods of time.

Conversely, for a time, there can be high morale in an organization without proficiency and organizational discipline. However, a lack of proficiency and organizational discipline will eventually lead to chaos, never allowing the organization to reach its goals.

High morale by itself will not allow an organization to attain its goals. However, it will confirm that, if the organization is meeting its standards and expectations, then the leader is using positive, forceful leadership.

Chapter 5

LEADERSHIP REALITIES

A "reality" usually defines a condition that exists, but here realities are used to shift your paradigm, to make you view leadership from perspectives that may seem unfamiliar. A few of these realities may seem obvious, but they certainly weren't to me initially. They weren't taught to me either, but as I learned them, my leadership style changed. They are true in almost all situations.

1. **EVERYBODY WANTS TO BE ON A GOOD TEAM**

2. **PEOPLE DO WHAT THEY KNOW**

3. **DEFINED STANDARDS ARE EASIER FOR THE LEADER AND THE LED**

4. **THERE IS AUTHORITY AND THEN THERE IS POWER**

5. **THE JUNIOR MUST ADJUST TO THE SENIOR**

6. **EVEN GOOD CHANGE CREATES FRICTION**

7. **EVERYBODY WANTS TO BE TREATED WITH RESPECT**

8. **YOUR WAY IS NOT THE ONLY WAY**

9. **MONEY MATTERS**

10. **IN THE ABSENCE OF AFFIRMATIVE LEADERSHIP, SOMEONE ELSE WILL FILL THE VOID**

1. EVERYBODY WANTS TO BE ON A GOOD TEAM

No one shows up on the first day and says "I think I'll be the worst employee I can be." It just doesn't happen. Most people want to work for a company in order to provide for life's necessities, to connect with a certain community, or possibly to improve themselves. Some people join organizations, such as non-profits, in order to further a cause in which they believe. In any case, absolutely no one joins a company or an organization to do a bad job. No matter what circumstances caused a person to join a company or an organization, a person inevitably walks in the door wanting to do a good job for what he hopes is a top-notch outfit. Poor performance is usually a learned, or even worse, an expected behavior.

The very important corollary to this thought is that *good people want to be around other good people*. They do not want to belong to an organization that tolerates bad behavior or lack of direction, and they will actively seek to move out of the organization if at all possible. This has enormous implications for volunteer organizations, but also impacts for-profit companies if the economy is doing well.

Therefore, it is incumbent upon the leader of any organization to realize he must strive to develop a good team that people actively seek out. This means setting realistic standards of behavior and objectives for productivity; good, motivated workers find standards and objectives comforting because they are not ambiguous. It also means creating a positive atmosphere where people feel comfortable to work and develop. Ideally, employees should want to come to work because the work environment is enjoyable. A good work environment also enhances performance.

If you don't create the proper work environment, then your good, talented people will leave as soon as another opportunity presents itself.

If I ever had another "light bulb" moment in leadership, this was it:

As the Commanding Officer of a recruiting station, I had a number of very competent recruiters. However, I was being forced to accept as a sub-station commander a senior non-commissioned officer (Staff NCO in the Marines) who had burned too many bridges at another recruiting station in the Midwest.

Within the first month, this new Staff NCO committed an ethics violation. As was my custom with sensitive issues, I discussed this matter with my trusted advisors, one of whom was my senior recruiter trainer. He was an exceptionally professional Marine with a great sense of humor. When I asked him what he thought I should do, he looked me dead in the eye and said "Sir, I don't want to belong to a unit that would have a guy like him in it."

That got my attention. I realized right then that if I did not deal with the unethical behavior, I would soon be losing the trust and respect of all my very competent, professional Staff NCO's. Certainly, performance throughout the command would suffer.

I had multiple courses of action available to me, but I did what I thought was right for all concerned. The disciplinary action I took allowed the Marines to maintain pride in their unit, thereby saving the performance and morale of the command. Once my senior recruiter trainer told me he did not want to belong to a unit with unethical personnel, the choice was clear, because everybody wants to be on a good team.

2. PEOPLE DO WHAT THEY KNOW

I no longer believe that people or organizations do things because they have studied and weighed the alternatives and come up with the best way. Naively, I assumed this for many years, but then I started to notice a pattern of someone coming along and saying "Why don't we look at it this way?" People do what they know how to do, and they probably do it well; but there may be a better way to do things. To effect change, the leader needs to change what they know.

Sometimes cost savings or a need for increased customer satisfaction drive these initiatives, but sometimes it is an outsider, a new employee with a fresh perspective, or perhaps an enterprising worker already in the department who can see a better way. In any case, driving this change is the leader's job; in effect, you must use your leadership position to change what the organization knows.

However, a great new idea may not be practical and, most likely, those who do the actual work will be able to point that out. Listen to them. *To effect proper change, it is least effective to just order new methods or procedures. It is most effective to bring all stakeholders into the discussion, in order to explain why the change is necessary, why it will be beneficial, and to get valuable input.* This will lessen resistance to change. (See Reality # 6 below).

This applies on an individual basis as well. The sentiments most often expressed by frustrated leaders is: "I can't believe he doesn't know that." or "Should I have to tell her that?" I've heard these phrases literally hundreds of times. Usually, my reply is "Have you told him exactly what you expect?"

In most cases, people should be aware of the obvious, but it really depends on their previous experience. I remember working in a hospital at a young age and my supervisor told everyone to punch out on the time clock within five minutes of the end of the shift, which was 8:30 PM. I started punching out at 8:26 and 8:27, oblivious to the fact that no one else was punching out with me. I had to be told specifically that she meant before 8:35 PM. I just didn't know.

It is shortsighted to assume that all methods and ideas have been tried and found wanting, or that people are not intelligent enough for the job. More than likely, the opposite is true. *People do what they know; if necessary, change what they know.*

3. DEFINED STANDARDS ARE EASIER FOR THE LEADER AND THE LED

Good leaders use their influence to set, change, and enforce standards. I have found that the clarity of well-defined standards makes everyone on the team think more clearly and innovatively. Also, well-defined standards reduce tension in the workplace because everyone knows what the common objectives are. The standards become a unifying force. If the three indicators of effective leadership (Proficiency, Organizational Discipline, and High Morale) are not present in your department, first look at what the standards are, whether they are realistic, and whether there are mechanisms to enforce them.

Standards (sometimes called objectives) need to be realistic, enforceable, and in line with higher level organizational standards and goals.* The standards should also stretch the capability of the department so that attaining the standards has real meaning. You will find that higher standards normally require more resources (people, money, technology, etc.), so align your standards in accordance with your department's true capabilities. Stretch your team, but do not break it.

With very rare exception, 100% is not a realistic standard. An organization that mandates 100% as its standard across the board will have a poor-performing unit with low morale. There is no way to enforce 100% as a standard unless everyone who comes up short gets dismissed; but then there would not be an organization.

Do not be afraid to change standards. When you examine forced changes of leadership due to poor performance, the new leader is brought in primarily to set or change standards and then to enforce them. Good leaders understand that groups of people usually do only what is expected of them. Keep an eye on where your larger organization is going and refine your standards as necessary so that there is not a forced change in your department.

There is an old management phrase, "If you can't count it, you can't improve it." In the vast majority of situations, this is true. Even if you improve something as subjective as the attitude of some employees, this should show up in increased productivity. Define your standards and enforce them. Your department will run much better.

---

* Goals are normally broader than standards/objectives, and perhaps unreachable, but something that a higher level organization or enterprise might strive for, such as "always exceeding our customers' expectations."

4. THERE IS AUTHORITY AND THEN THERE IS POWER

In most large organizations, there are charts or wire diagrams that presumably dictate levels of authority. At each level, there is a usually a limit as to how far such things as approvals, discipline, budget, or hiring decisions can be handled. You may be in a position that clearly defines your level of authority. However, once in a while, you may make a decision well within your authority that will be overridden. This may be from your immediate senior, or from many levels up in the organization.

You can either accept it or fight it, citing your authority. In any case, *assume that the "power" is acting in accordance with the best intentions of the organization.* This is normally true, but worrying whether it is true or not will not help you. Do not become annoyed because someone who may be far removed from you used her power to usurp your authority. Also, do not assume you made a bad decision. Presumably, you consulted with your immediate senior and others upon whom you could count for good guidance, and then made the best decision for your department.

Take the high road, attempt to find out the reason without negative overtones, and then move on. The use of power is normal in large organizations. Understand it, do not decry it.

5. THE JUNIOR MUST ADJUST TO THE SENIOR

Every leader develops her own way to properly influence people to get the job done. As I said in the Introduction, I've seen all types of leaders from varying backgrounds and personalities. As long as the leadership style is ethical, legal, moral, <u>and effective</u>, everyone will have to adjust to that style.

A junior leader must assume that the immediate senior leader and those on up the chain have more responsibilities, and hence more stress than the junior leader herself. They also probably put in more time. Do not fall into the mental trap of complaining that senior leaders have less to do, "they don't know what junior personnel do," or other such comments. It is a negative mindset that is never productive for anyone. With rare exception, it is also not true.

Therefore, if a senior leader has more responsibility and stress, and less time, it is incumbent on the junior leader to adjust or compensate for a senior leader's style. At a minimum, if there are seriously conflicting styles, the junior leader must come to some sort of accommodation. A senior leader should not be put into the position of having to worry about a junior leader's attitude and her ability to get the job done. If there must be a meeting of the minds to resolve styles, the junior leader should initiate the meeting, because more than likely, the senior leader is either not aware of the conflict in style, or the senior leader, noting poor performance on the part of the junior leader, is wondering not what's wrong, but <u>whether he should be replacing the junior leader</u>. As I say in a later chapter, if you have the interest, you have the responsibility.

If you disagree on substantive material versus just style, meet with the senior leader and discuss it. If, after hearing the rationale, you still disagree, it is your responsibility to carry out the senior leader's wishes as if you completely agreed with his position.

In the military, this is a maxim. Junior leaders get their say on the course of action, indeed it is incumbent on senior leaders to solicit input. However, once the boss makes the decision, everybody leaves the room supporting that decision. If you think it through, it is the only way that makes sense to keep an organization running well. Otherwise, morale within an organization will fracture.

Along your career path, you will always have senior leaders with whom you disagree either in style or substance. You can and should make your thoughts known, but you must also support the senior leader when executing your job. If you can not support the senior leader, then it may be time to move on, either within or outside the organization.

6. EVEN GOOD CHANGE CREATES FRICTION

Whenever I talk about leadership to a group, I usually ask people to examine their leadership style in reference to the following statements:

"If it ain't broke, don't fix it"

and

"Change isn't necessary;
survival isn't mandatory"

The first quote was fairly popular in the 1980's and was the rule at many well-run organizations. The second quote is paraphrased from management guru W. Edwards Deming. I used to believe that the first quote was far more applicable to most organizations, but it is really a trap and is also a lazy, naïve way to lead.

My experience tells me that *change will come whether we want it to or not*. If change is not coming directly from within the organization, then factors outside of an organization, such as technological improvements, trends, or competitors will certainly change the dynamic within the organization. There is a terrific book called *Who Moved My Cheese?* by Spencer Johnson that has become somewhat of a business classic. It is a story about how people (actually mice in the book) either see change coming and prepare for it, or they ignore change hoping it will never occur and then suffer the consequences. I highly recommend this book; it only takes an hour or so to read.

Leaders need to know that *friction will occur no matter how well-planned or explained the change is.* Friction is not good or bad, it is just an issue that must be managed. There may be people who wonder if their jobs are at risk, despite previous reassurance. If a worker perceives that her ability to pay the mortgage or put food on the table is in jeopardy, she will bring a different attitude into the workplace. Also, there are almost always some people who will put the ultimate negative spin on a positive change with "What was wrong with the old way? We did it that way for years." Negative influences can be seductive early on and they can infect the attitudes of many people.

Leaders must be aware that changes in attitudes will occur, some subtle, some not, and they must deal with them as they arise. Knowing the people well will allow a leader to more readily see or anticipate changes in attitude. Also, *you should be visible and approachable immediately upon the implementation of any change in the work environment; this will be a calming influence.* You must plan to be more visible than usual the next few days. Never think that once a change is decided upon and implemented that everything will be fine. It does not work that way.

Change is going to come. It is inevitable. Make your department and organization better by seeing it coming, planning for it, and executing the necessary changes smoothly. If you do not, survival may be in doubt.

7. EVERYBODY WANTS TO BE TREATED WITH RESPECT

There are many leaders out there who believe that creating a harsh, high stress environment is the only way to lead. However, I believe that *every employee, from the CEO to the newest temporary worker, wants to be treated with respect.* Throughout my career, this has been a constant in every country, work environment, and social setting. Courtesy, understanding, and encouragement are welcome in any situation and enable a leader to maximize efforts and results from juniors, seniors, and peers alike. Conversely, when a leader routinely exhibits anger, degrading language, and a disdain for understanding, an organization can not hope to succeed over a period of time.

In my Marine Corps career, I saw far too many officers who treated different ranks with different levels of respect. As a young captain, I was in a fairly independent position where I had to interact with all different levels and types of people. For a particular issue, I had to talk to a major but the major's assistant, when I identified myself as Captain Ballard, always said the major was not available. (This was before voice mail). I started to suspect it was my lower rank. So I called him one day and again he was not available. Within seconds, I had another major that I worked with call him and he just happened to be there. By not treating me with respect, that major lost the respect of many other people, including those who could help him with his career.

Once I became more experienced in the Marines, I treated privates through generals with the same tone of voice and level of respect. I heard more than once how much this was appreciated, particularly from the lower ranks. <u>This is not to say that a leader relinquishes his role as the standard bearer and loses his need to discipline</u>, but if most people want to do the right thing and want to be on a good team, then treating everyone with a certain level of respect will pay huge dividends for both you and your team.

You cannot talk to higher management one way and lower level employees another way. The hypocrisy is or will be easily visible and will make <u>you</u> unworthy of respect by all levels in the organization. If leadership is the ability to successfully influence people to achieve an outcome, and you don't have the respect of the people you are trying to influence by virtue of your hypocrisy, your job will be very difficult at best.

There is a strain of leadership that recommends upon taking over a new organization to be firmer in the beginning so that employees learn your standards quickly. You can then ease to the level that will maintain those standards. There is merit to this strain of leadership; it is the degree of firmness with which you must be careful. It is certainly true that firming up your leadership style after an initial period of a looser style is very difficult, if not impossible, but always treat everyone with respect. Respect towards you will increase accordingly.

8. YOUR WAY IS NOT THE ONLY WAY

Presumably, senior leaders have seen positive qualities in you making them believe that you can be a solid leader who will help the organization. However, just because you have been tapped as a leader does not necessarily mean that you have improved your intelligence or that you have been rewarded with additional insight. It does mean that you now have a chance to positively influence people and that you have a responsibility to get the job done and to take care of the people under your charge.

When I discuss Anticipatory Initiative in Chapter 6, I mention bringing ideas from other disciplines into your work area. Similarly, many people around you have great ideas. They may be junior to you, may be a senior mentor, or even a friend from another organization. Your leadership position gives you the ability to implement ideas from everywhere; <u>they do not have to be your ideas</u>. *Good leaders use their authority to implement ideas, no matter the source.*

You should publicly acknowledge those within your organization who give you great suggestions. It helps build morale within the work force, but it also, very importantly, lets people know that they can have an influence on bettering the work environment. An additional bonus is that you may be inundated with other suggested improvements.

Do not worry about giving credit where credit is due. Most senior leaders will not make the mistake of thinking that the person with a good idea should necessarily be the leader of that department. Planning for and implementing an idea is normally far more complex than just having the idea; there are usually ramifications for other departments, nuances that must be addressed, and so on. Most senior leaders understand this. Your job as a leader is to use your influence for the betterment of the organization. Be open to suggestions no matter the source.

As a warning, if two people know something, it is not a secret. If you do pass an idea off as your own, you will likely be found out. It also violates integrity and you will lose the trust of both juniors and seniors. When you get an idea, no matter the source, use your position to do the right thing.

9. MONEY MATTERS

In every organization, money matters. From non-profits to commercial businesses, from athletic organizations to government offices, money matters because the bills must be paid. There are usually two types of people in an organization, those who bring in money such as salesmen, grant writers, or those who allocate higher-level funds, and those who perform necessary functions but essentially spend the money internally, such as distribution, administration, athletic teams, facility management, and the like. In commercial organizations, salesmen bring to the bottom line only the profit margin, but when the internal spenders save a dollar, the dollar drops to the bottom line.

Every enterprise needs capable leadership when leading these two types of people, and you must know where your organization fits into the overall money picture. There are usually targets/objectives to bring in money and a budget to execute all activities, sales or otherwise. If you do not understand your particular situation, then you should ask. If your department is far enough down the chain that you do not have to worry about your particular budget, become informed about the higher level budget, because at some point it will affect you.

If you are not aware of the overall money picture and how you fit into it, you may be looked upon as naïve or "out of the loop." Senior leaders may assume you do not have the skills to understand. None of these scenarios are favorable to you.

Get in the loop. Money matters.

10. IN THE ABSENCE OF AFFIRMATIVE LEADERSHIP, SOMEONE ELSE WILL FILL THE VOID

People want to be led. They may say they want to do their own thing or that they hate their boss, but the truth is they want to be led by men and women of integrity and competence who possess a positive, forceful leadership style. Never forget this. There will be times when you will have people test this reality, but the vast majority of people want to be led well. *Without exception, whenever I saw an authorized leader fail to exercise affirmative leadership, someone else filled the void.* It has happened to me and I've seen it happen to many other leaders.

People must know you are in charge of your department <u>without you having to declare it verbally</u>. Your leadership presence must be felt whether you are physically present or not. You can best do this by exhibiting the traits and executing the principles outlined in the next two chapters. If you have to tell your department that you are in charge, then you have a serious credibility issue.

Two things can happen if you fail to adequately fill your leadership role. The first is that a good person in your department who does not aspire to be the leader will fill the gap in your leadership and keep the department running well enough. However, if your boss is inspecting what he is expecting (see Principle # 3 in Chapter 7), then he will wonder why you are the leader of the department.

The second and most likely thing to happen is a negative influence will emerge to fill the gap. The reason a negative influence is more likely to arise is that the generally positive people will hold back still waiting to be led, while the negative influence will be more vocal. This is not to say that generally good people will all follow the negative influence, but at the least, it will be a serious disruption in the work environment. If the situation lingers, the negative influence can become the dominant leadership presence. That is not good for you or the organization.

Exercise your affirmative leadership by understanding the traits and principles required. If you do not, someone else will exert leadership influence, for good or bad.

Chapter 6

LEADERSHIP TRAITS

The definition of "trait" is "a distinguishing quality." The traits I list and comment on below are those that I believe are the distinguishing qualities of the best leaders I have known, observed, or studied.

No one exhibits all of these traits at the optimum level; some people may be quite inept at them initially. I still struggle with some of these traits and must consciously remind myself that leading requires constant self-development. These traits can be learned; indeed you should be learning about them throughout your life.

As an adult, your choices determine the outcome of your life. You may have to overcome some of your natural tendencies or habits. However, if you want to become the best leader possible, develop these traits.

1. **INTEGRITY** - **Uprightness of character and soundness of moral and ethical principles**

2. **COMPETENCE** – **The synergy of knowledge and judgment necessary to gain the confidence of your seniors, juniors, and peers**

3. **DEPENDABILITY** – **The certainty of the proper performance of tasks and responsibilities**

4. **ENERGY** – **The mental and physical stamina required to accomplish one's responsibilities**

5. **OPTIMISM** – **An inclination to anticipate the best possible outcome**

6. **DECISIVENESS** – **The ability to reach timely decisions and to communicate them in a clear, understandable manner**

7. **TACT** – **The ability to deal directly with others without creating offense**

8. **PRESENCE** – The ability to garner respect by one's personal conduct, bearing, and appearance

9. **LOYALTY** - Faithfulness to the organization, your seniors, and juniors

10. **ANTICIPATORY INITIATIVE** – Seeing what has to be done and commencing a course of action, sometimes even before the action is deemed necessary

Note: "Intelligence" as a trait is assumed. In most organizations, you would not have been placed in a responsible leadership position without the level of intelligence required to get the job done.

1. INTEGRITY - Uprightness of character and soundness of moral and ethical principles

Leaders are and should be held to a higher standard of integrity. People do not want to follow men or women of low integrity, and will usually only do so out of some fear. This is because there is a general consensus of right and wrong and most people want to do the right thing and want to be around people who feel the same way. Therefore, leaders of known low integrity have great difficulty inspiring loyalty and trust in people. *Integrity must be part of the person; it can not be a workplace habit.*

There are many components to integrity. The obvious elements of integrity are <u>truthfulness</u> and <u>honesty</u>. Lying on statistics, about promotion opportunities, or the like will place a leader as someone whose word can not be trusted. This mistrust will not be relegated to just the subject you lied about, but about everything that you say from then on. As I said in the last chapter, if two people know something, then there is no secret. It is difficult to positively influence people when they do not believe anything you say.

Cheating on such things as work processes or promotion exams are dangerous to the organization. For instance, authorizing a manufacturing shortcut on a consumer product may lead to safety and liability issues that can shut down the company due to a lawsuit. Cheating on an exam does not allow the organization to put the best qualified people in the proper positions. People know cheating is wrong and you will not be able to lead them successfully if they find out you cheated.

Stealing is a serious issue that can be covered up for some time. It occurs, it lowers morale, but those who know about it are sometimes reluctant to come forward. In some cases, that reluctance may be understandable, but it is still frustrating. If leaders are stealing or know about theft and do nothing, the leader's influence is greatly reduced. Most people do not want to be around thieves, nor do they want to be led by people who tolerate theft.

The deeper, less obvious elements of integrity consist of <u>justice, unselfishness,</u> and <u>moral courage</u>.

Justice is the ability to be impartial and consistent in the exercise of leadership responsibilities. These responsibilities include both the reward and discipline sides of leadership. I once interviewed a man for a supervisor position who proudly said that, at his previous company, he bent the rules for a good worker even though the worker had been involved in multiple fights, which were strictly against that company's policy. He repeated this story to other people within my facility and none of us could quite believe he was proud of it. The man did not possess impartial and consistent justice and he did not get the job.

Unselfishness entails avoiding the trap of providing for one's own comfort and personal goals at the expense of others. Upon taking a leadership position, do not make moves that appear to provide for your comfort (such as taking a co-worker's desk and chair) just because you now can. You must get across that the department will work together and not worry about largely meaningless assets. This is not to say do not set up your office, cubicle or whatever, to most effectively lead your department, just do not appear selfish about it. If it is not critical to effectiveness and efficiency, try not to rearrange assets to suit your personal comfort.

There are usually some perks to leadership, but they are largely recognition of the additional stress that comes with leadership, or at the very highest levels, an acknowledgement of the unique skills required for such positions. Do not abuse the perks and definitely do not flaunt them to those junior to you.

Moral courage is the willingness to always do the right thing despite the consequences. Owning up to your mistakes or taking an unpopular stand can be very difficult at times, but it will garner you immense respect over the long haul.

Remember that *the level of respect accorded you is based on more than just your position.* Without integrity, all is for naught. People simply do not want to follow leaders of low integrity.

2. COMPETENCE - The synergy of knowledge and judgment necessary to gain the confidence of your seniors, juniors, and peers

There is a train of thought that one can not lead an organization unless one technically knows what that organization does, that is, one can perform all of the processes or functions that the people in the organization do. Logically, this train of thought assumes that no senior leader can emerge unless he starts at the very bottom and becomes competent at all of the required tasks in that organization. That is obviously not true.

Most of the senior leadership in the U.S. military started as Second Lieutenants (Ensigns for the Navy and Coast Guard) fresh out of college in charge of a department that they get some training in, but certainly do not know in depth by any stretch. Instead, the military emphasizes leadership to its young officers, instilling values, behavioral norms, traits, and principles. Most either have successful careers or they leave early in their work career to pursue other opportunities. It is not a coincidence that young men and women still in their twenties who served in the military, and who may not have strong technical skills, are much sought after not only by business, but almost all professions. Why is this?

They are sought after because businesses and other organizations know that these young men and women can learn the technical duties as required, but they will exhibit sound leadership from day one.

Leadership competence is different than technical competence. Leadership competence requires that you constantly refine your ability to positively influence people. It also requires that you clearly understand the goals of your organization and the role it plays in the overall enterprise. Without this knowledge, you will be operating in a vacuum and will be less effective as a leader because you will lose touch with other departments and their leaders.

It also entails understanding enough technically to be able to direct your employees knowledgeably. You can learn the technical side prior to or just after assuming the leadership role. It is a rare organization that somehow does not allow for this learning to occur either through training or by allowing you to show initiative by learning the technical side on your own.

<u>This technical side includes those administrative duties required of the position</u>, not just the technical job function. I have seen too many leaders fail because they understood their employees' job functions but failed to perform their own required administrative duties. In most organizations, administrative excellence is required of leaders.

Finally, learn about leadership through books such as this, talking to other leaders, and keenly observing other organizations. Leadership competence is a constant learning process. *If you have been leading people without learning about leadership from other sources besides your own experience, then you are most likely underperforming as a leader and cheating your organization and your employees out of your best effort.* Reading about other leaders and other leadership philosophies can only help you and your organization.

3. DEPENDABILITY - The certainty of the proper performance of tasks and responsibilities

Bosses expect that once tasks or objectives are explained or understood, you will use all of the tools at your disposal to accomplish those tasks or objectives. In addition, people who work for you expect you to do what is necessary to accomplish assigned tasks or objectives. They also want to succeed.

No organization works in a vacuum. There are other people and departments counting on each other to get the job done. You do not have to know or do everything; however, you must understand that *all of the organizations involved, higher, lower, and adjacent, are expecting your department to do its job and do it well.* That is why you must acquire those tools necessary to successfully influence people to get the job done well and on time.

It is a pleasure for a senior leader to have a junior leader who can be given a task and then be relied upon to complete it on time while exceeding expectations. Anyone who has ever had junior leaders assigned to them can attest to this. It saves the senior leader much time and energy by not having to worry about a low-performing department, or spending extra time supervising a junior leader. Senior leaders do expect to be asked for help by junior leaders, but there is a line between asking for help and being spoon-fed.

When given a task, get it done on time while exceeding expectations. Get help if you need it, but ask for the help early enough to still allow you to finish on time.

4. ENERGY - The mental and physical stamina required to accomplish one's responsibilities

I once had a Marine boss in the mid 1990's who told me he thought the leader was the "energy" of an organization. I certainly did not buy that thought at the time, but as time went on, I began to observe the energy level of leaders. As I said in the Introduction, I've seen successful leaders who were outgoing and some who were more reserved; however, *every successful leader had a level of energy about him that came through no matter his personality.*

The Marine trait that is its nearest equivalent is "Enthusiasm – the display of sincere interest in the execution of one's responsibilities." However, I think more is required than just sincere interest. You simply must have sufficient mental and physical stamina to accomplish your assigned duties. Influencing people can be mentally draining on an individual, particularly an introvert. For some, the mental drain can lead to physical exhaustion as well.

Below in the Principles chapter, I talk about knowing yourself. Maintaining the proper amount of energy to accomplish your duties is about knowing yourself. You must have enough self-knowledge to properly care for yourself. That sounds almost too simple, but at times, I've strayed from taking care of myself when absorbed in getting the job done. I remember like it was yesterday having a talk with myself six months into my job as a Commanding Officer. I had to determine if the command was going to run me or if I was going to run the command. Difficult, stressful jobs can make you lose your energy quickly. Then you are of little value to the organization.

Importantly, your people can immediately read your energy level; you can not fake it. They will know if you are not up to the demands of leadership, or whether you have a sincere interest in both getting the job done and taking care of them.

I saw a television show recently where a very famous business leader was asked what he looks for in a more junior leader. He said that, intelligence being a given, energy was the most important requirement. That was a very telling comment. It is true that when your mind is fully in the game, you are a much more effective leader. Your energy level determines how much your mind is in the game.

5. OPTIMISM - An inclination to anticipate the best possible outcome

It is very easy to dismiss optimism as an important leadership trait. So many motivational gurus trumpet optimistic thinking as a virtue that it has almost become too cliché. However, I was lucky enough to hear Rudy Guiliani speak in March of 2004 and he said something that really hit home with me, "People don't follow pessimists." That is certainly true. In all my years of leading people and being around other leaders, I can not think of one successful leader who did not believe good things could or would happen.

As I have mentioned, in the absence of a strong positive message being sent to a group of people, a negative, easy-to-believe influence likely will arise. That negative influence will spread some discontent, but the group does not want to follow that messenger. They instinctively know it is not the correct path, because *people expect to be led by optimists.*

Thinking optimistically, however, must be followed up by acting optimistically. There should be a plan; there should be proactive, positive communication about the plan; there should be reasoned action. Thinking and then acting optimistically will greatly help you in successfully influencing your organization.

If a leader thinks the worst is going to happen, then the worst will likely happen, because people have difficulty letting a pessimistic leader succeed. If the leader believes and then plans for good things to happen, the group is very likely to succeed. If obstacles are in the way (and there are always some), work through them, or go over or around them. People want to succeed.

6. DECISIVENESS - The ability to reach timely decisions and to communicate them in a clear, understandable manner

Decisiveness is a time-saver, particularly for your employees. I am not suggesting that a leader hurry a decision just to show decisiveness. I am saying that once a decision has been made, announce it, explain the rationale if necessary, and then supervise that decision. If you wait too long to announce an important decision, then you will be creating unnecessary uncertainty that may result in unintended consequences. Negative rumors can start, junior leaders may make decisions that will contradict your upcoming decision, or other negative effects caused by delaying an announcement may arise.

Many leaders are taught to act in crisis situations if they are 60-70% sure of making the correct decision, because acting within a certain time frame may be more important than the actual decision itself. Although there are fast-moving situations in most organizations, there is usually adequate time to prepare and to be more than 60-70% sure of a major decision, especially if you have thought through the "what ifs" prior to making the decision.

Assemble the stakeholders, get their input, think through the issues, get mentoring if necessary, tell your boss what you are thinking, make your decision, and then announce it as promptly as possible. You may have to "pre-announce" it to a small group (perhaps the stakeholders) but <u>if it is your decision, they must keep your decision private until you announce it.</u> A leader cannot have any "spin" put on his decision prior to the actual announcement.

Consistent decisiveness creates confidence in you, both from seniors and juniors. Employees may disagree with a particular decision, but they will know you are doing what you think is right. That is valuable by itself as it will make employees believe that they are in good hands. Even if your decision proves to be wrong, just re-trace your process, communicate your re-thinking to all the appropriate parties, and move forward.

7. TACT - The ability to deal directly with others without creating offense

Every leader should be able to talk directly and on point to juniors, seniors, and peers. This is particularly important when dealing with personnel issues. Leaders always have to deal with difficult personnel issues, but even the most unreasonable people eventually understand if spoken to directly, calmly, and firmly. Most people appreciate the feedback if done so honestly and directly.

The tactful leader will do this by focusing on the behavior and not on the person. It is easier for someone to understand that he must correct a behavior, rather than change his personality. Attempting to correct a personality will likely breed resentment, not improvement, and it is seriously frowned upon by almost all human relations departments in large organizations. For instance, telling someone that he must stop yelling in the workplace is alright; telling someone he is a hothead will not correct anything. If further disciplinary measures are necessary, then you have direct evidence of a behavior, not an interpretation of a personality. If dismissal becomes necessary, you will be on much firmer legal ground addressing behaviors.

Much like decisiveness, tact is a time saver. People who must be counseled in some way need to be told how you feel in as plain language as possible. Anything else will just drag on the dilemma. Initially, everyone wants to do a good job, but sometimes events in organizations reveal deficient behaviors in individuals that must be addressed. Addressing them earlier rather than later will help the employee correct the behaviors more readily, and morale in the workplace will be improved as employees know that you will swiftly deal with less than appropriate behavior.

When dealing with seniors and peers, again address behavior directly with examples if at all possible. Being more conversational than with a junior employee may be appropriate, but get to the point.

If you have trouble with word phrasing, body language, or other behaviors that affect your ability to be tactful, seek out a trusted mentor or peer to assist you, using role play if necessary. Being direct yet tactful requires experience; the more you practice, the better you become at it.

8. PRESENCE - The ability to garner respect by one's personal conduct, bearing and appearance

In the Introduction, I said "I have seen great leaders who were very outgoing and those who were quiet and reserved. Some strictly followed the rule book; others couldn't find the rule book and had no desire to do so. Some were extremely humble, some not so humble." It is true that almost any personality type can be an effective leader, but no matter the personality, *a leader's presence must be felt.* By your actions and words, you must reassure everyone involved that you are up to the task.

Presence is a difficult trait to tangibly describe, but ultimately it comes down to peers, juniors, and seniors recognizing you as the authority within your own department, whether you are physically there or not. Many of the traits and principles in this book will help you achieve presence within your department, but there are also other attributes necessary to achieve a positive presence.

Day to day, you should be <u>calm</u>, <u>approachable</u>, and <u>visible</u> when physically at work. Regarding calm, I have yet to observe a great leader who routinely rants and raves as part of his leadership style. A visibly high stress leadership style engenders great tension into the work environment and employees will never perform to their optimum, nor will they want to. Usually, high stress leaders believe they are doing the right thing largely because that is what they have seen before in other leaders (See Reality #2). They never realize that if the employees stay, they are largely tuning the leader out and accomplishing the minimum tasks required. Innovation and creative thinking will be nonexistent. In a low unemployment economy, the good workers will simply leave.

Calm is especially important in a crisis. There will be plenty of people overreacting to any number of situations and rumors. If you add to the confusion by panicking, you will not be able to think your way out of the situation. Your department will be looking to you for guidance and a path, not more panic. Reassure your department and those around you. Great leaders, under crisis, think more clearly, rationally, and innovatively than at normal times.

You should always be approachable. If an employee feels uncomfortable in talking to you or believes that talking to you is the same as talking to a wall, then the department may get the minimum job done, but it will not excel and innovate. It is even worse if you are known to have a short temper. Most people simply do not want to be around angry people for any length of time and will eventually avoid doing so. Most people can tolerate some anger and tension, but almost everyone

Leadership Traits

will eventually wear down mentally and emotionally in a constantly angry and negative environment.

For visibility, if you have a separate office but are physically at work, you need to ensure that you practice Management by Walking Around (MBWA). I'm not sure where the term originated, but it is a very good practice. Your employees need to physically see you in their area throughout the day. It engenders trust and confidence in you.

If done effectively, MBWA combined with a theory called Servant Leadership, contributes greatly to a positive presence. Servant Leadership, advocated by Robert Greenleaf, founder of the Center for Servant-Leadership in Indianapolis, largely teaches that the truly effective leader has a servant mentality; it emphasizes ethics, collaboration, trust, and listening. The leader may have the goal or vision in mind, but he needs to enable his employees to achieve their goals and help with the organizational goals also. The leader should be asking questions largely along the line of "Do you have everything you need?" or "How can we improve?" Well developed questioning and listening skills contribute greatly to your presence.

Also, excellent <u>speaking skills</u> contribute to your presence. Employees usually like to see their leader speak publicly; it gives them additional confidence in you. You can be effective within your department if your public speaking skills are marginal, but you will not advance much further within the organization. You definitely will not be called upon to give presentations to senior leaders, whom you may want to get to know.

If you want to advance, practice your speaking skills. For marginal to fair speakers, I highly recommend joining a Toastmasters group. Toastmasters is an excellent, low-pressure environment in which to help improve your speaking skills.

<u>Never complain openly</u>. A leader is always a conduit between upper and lower levels and complaining about one or the other levels positions <u>you</u> as the problem, not the solution provider. As a leader, you will discuss sensitive personnel or other work issues with your bosses, but do it in a constructive, positive manner. Be seen as the solution provider, not the whiner.

Definitely, *do not show disrespect to senior leaders in front of your people*. You would be violating the trust and confidence of senior leaders who put you in your leadership position. You would also be eroding morale within the organization as employees may think they have poor senior leaders. Also, not only will your own department know what you said, but, most likely, within one day, so will all of the other nearby departments. It is a no-win situation all the way around. Do not complain openly.

Lastly, <u>appearance</u> also contributes to presence. There are many people who feel that appearance should not matter, but we are largely a visual species and we react to what we see. Without belaboring the point, practice what is generally considered good grooming and dress one level up from your position.

I knew a fabulous worker at one company, but his clothes, hair and beard were largely out of control and no matter what good work he did, the senior boss at the facility would not consider him for promotion based on his appearance. When this man's supervisor told him he would not be considered for other opportunities due to his appearance, he tucked in his shirt, got a nice haircut, and trimmed his facial hair. Within six months, he was a team leader and within a year was universally recognized as a go-to guy in the entire facility. Should it be that way? Maybe not, but it is that way.

9. LOYALTY - Faithfulness to the organization, your seniors and juniors

Loyalty is necessary in some form for an effective work environment. Today's job-hopping mentality would seem to make loyalty almost a forgotten element of leadership, but that is not the case. Even if one is not in a leadership position, there is always some sense of loyalty to the company or to the individual who did the hiring, and usually some sense of loyalty to fellow workers.

However, *to be an effective leader, you must be loyal up and down the chain.* To be selected for a position of leadership means that you have already exhibited some kind of loyalty to the organization. It helps if your organization has a noble, humanitarian purpose, but most organizations are not that way, so loyalty may be more of a personal issue. If so, it then becomes incumbent on the very senior leaders of the organization to inspire loyalty downward in order to keep good people within the organization.

Once you are in that position of leadership, you must quickly demonstrate your loyalty, not only to the overall organization, but also to your department. There are many ways of accomplishing this, such as communicating proactively, listening well, and realizing everybody wants to be on a good team and acting accordingly. Your demonstration of loyalty will ensure that your employees know that you have their best interest, and that of the organization's, in mind.

I was always very loyal down the chain in all my endeavors, as I truly believed that most people want to do a good job. It worked for me. However, do not forget to show strong loyalty up the chain as well. Keeping in mind the enterprise's intent, ensure that you exhibit obvious loyalty to your immediate boss and the next higher level; they deserve it until proven otherwise.

10. ANTICIPATORY INITIATIVE - Seeing what has to be done and commencing a course of action, sometimes even before the action is deemed necessary

This is a trait that the absolutely best leaders possess. Most new leaders have the ability to see what has to be done and then do it without being directed to do so; presumably, this was a prerequisite to being placed into a position of leadership. Although this will make you a solid contributor to most organizations, truly great leaders understand there is more to initiative than just that. Using any combination of intuition, experience, brainstorming, or the like, *outstanding leaders anticipate required actions, usually before anyone else even knows an action may be required.*

Later in my Marine Corps career, I attended some higher level schools in Quantico and I remember a general with over 30 years of service talking to my class on why he thought some people went far in their particular field and others didn't. He believed that those who have the most success in a particular field "cast a wide net." That is, they study or read outside of their main field, enabling them to bring in outside theories or practices from other disciplines into their own field of endeavor or study. This makes a lot of sense to me.

It is easy to plod along and let experience alone be your teacher. However, an agile, anticipating mind would read not only about his own occupation, but also about many other areas. It does not just make you smarter or more interesting, it makes you think about your own field and how you might do it differently. It will help you introduce new ideas into your own line of work, even before you know you need those ideas. Combine this "casting a wide net" with a dependable, resourceful attitude, and you will have anticipatory initiative.

This is a learned trait; do not fall into the trap of thinking that some people have this anticipatory gift and others do not. It just requires curiosity, keen observation, and self-improvement capability.

Chapter 7

LEADERSHIP PRINCIPLES

A principle is a behavior to be executed routinely or a base of knowledge to be maintained and improved. Excellent leadership requires action. You should not only understand realities and exhibit traits, you must also act. The following principles form an excellent basis for leadership actions.

1. **KNOW YOURSELF**

2. **COMMUNICATE POSITIVELY AND PROACTIVELY**

3. **INSPECT WHAT YOU EXPECT**

4. **TEACH ETHICAL BEHAVIOR**

5. **EXECUTE A VISION/GO IN A DIRECTION**

6. **BE JOB-FOCUSED, NOT TIME-FOCUSED**

7. **TRAIN YOUR TEAM AS A TEAM**

8. **KNOW THE INTENTS/GOALS TWO LEVELS UP AND THE OPERATIONAL DETAILS TWO LEVELS DOWN**

9. **DEVELOP A SENSE OF RESPONSIBILITY IN YOUR PEOPLE**

10. **PRAISE IN PUBLIC, REPRIMAND IN PRIVATE**

1. KNOW YOURSELF

To lead others effectively, you must first know yourself. To do this effectively, you should fully understand your likes and dislikes, what angers you quickly, what makes you feel good or bad, and what are your biases. This takes active, reflective thought. This is absolutely essential for two reasons.

The first reason is that you will be able to modify your potentially extreme actions/reactions if you possess a strong self-understanding. For instance, if a colleague raises an issue that brings back a difficult memory or just makes you angry, you should be able to rationalize a solution rather than react out of anger or deep emotion. Calm, reflective thought can occur, rather than rash, potentially destructive actions.

The second reason is that, although it would be nice to keep all of your personality traits private, in reality, your people deserve to know those parts of your personality that will influence their work environment. For instance, if you have a ritual early in the morning that you perform to help you think appropriately throughout the day (such as coming in early to read the newspaper), you should tell your people this fact. Otherwise, upon your arrival at work, they may come into your office expecting your immediate attention on what they consider important matters, but in reality you will not be fully engaged. You will end up feeling angry for the interruption, but they will be angrier because their boss would not pay attention to what they considered a pressing issue.

This latter reason can not be a hard and fast rule, the exceptions being safety or extreme money matters due to downtime or similar circumstances, but in those instances where work routine is involved, you must let your people know your preferences, likes and dislikes, and habits that may affect their environment.

For most newer leaders, this is very difficult as they are still forming their leadership style and may not have a well defined sense of how they can most effectively lead. They simply have not experienced as many difficult situations as more experienced leaders have. However, *reflective thought, mentally putting yourself in difficult situations and imagining how you would react, will help fill the experience gap.*

2. COMMUNICATE POSITIVELY AND PROACTIVELY

You should *actively provide your people as much information as they can handle before issues arise or fester.* Even if you have worked only two months in your life, you know that information gets passed throughout a workforce completely without foundation. In the absence of real information, unfounded rumors will occur.

Being proactive and anticipatory about information requirements will do two things. First, it will prevent unfounded rumors from becoming problems because you will have provided accurate information beforehand. Second, it will enhance your authority as someone who knows what is going on. If you tell your employees what is going to happen before it actually happens, or address a sensitive issue that may soon emerge, your credibility will be enhanced. People will feel like their boss knows what is going on and cares enough to tell them. Remember though that personnel issues must remain private for both ethical and legal reasons.

It would be best to establish a pattern of communication, such as a weekly meeting, a morning pep talk, or the like. Do not wait to communicate when an event is already occurring. Be proactive and positive, not reactive and in a panic.

3. INSPECT WHAT YOU EXPECT

As a leader, you will have certain standards to strive for or objectives to accomplish. In larger enterprises, these are usually measured objectives; in smaller companies or organizations, they may just be understood. In any case, you will always give your department tasks to accomplish. There are two main points associated with this principle: employees understanding the tasks required and the setting of priorities.

Corporate trainers love to play a game where they whisper a phrase in the ear of an employee and have him pass it on to another person, who then passes it on to another, and so on until about five or six people have heard the phrase. The trainer then asks the last person to hear the phrase what was said. Inevitably, the phrase gets garbled as it moves from person to person.

This is actually what happens. It does not mean you have incompetent employees; it is just normal that people hear things differently and then pass them on differently. Also, it should not be news to anyone that most people may hear something, but do not truly listen and absorb what is being said. Many good leaders actually ask their people to repeat back the task just explained so that a clearer understanding occurs; however, if that task is further passed on, you can not be sure what is being said or heard.

Therefore it is incumbent upon you to *be very clear in your expectations* and then inspect what you expect in some way. In most cases, simply tactfully checking two levels down should suffice (or just one level if that person actually will perform the task). If it is a very critical task, you may want to set a time for a formal review of the task to ensure its accomplishment.

This should not be construed as micromanaging. Workers react to their leader's expectations and they are far more comfortable when they clearly know what is expected. *Checking up on what you expect is a very critical and necessary part of task accomplishment. Just because you tell someone to do something does not mean it is going to get done.*

The second point to remember about this principle is that not everything is a priority. Some leaders try to make 15-20 items "important." However, if you are seriously tracking more than 3-5 items, then you may have trouble identifying what is truly important. (This assumes that your senior leaders have not overburdened you).

This does not apply to monitoring or overseeing items. Even the smallest commercial companies have multiple financial issues they must track. Leaders of large organizations have dozens of items they must receive data on. I am talking about tasks for which someone is directly and closely responsible. If you have told your people that you will be closely watching for 20 items, then they will not be able to comprehend what is truly important. Perhaps you are the exceptional individual who has the type of mind that can do this, but most of your workers are not the type who can place your perceived importance on this many items. You would be setting them up for failure and will soon incur morale problems.

Inspect what you expect, but ensure that the items are truly important.

4. TEACH ETHICAL BEHAVIOR

You must actively communicate the expected ethical behavior. Many new leaders assume that people working with or for them have the same set of values as they do. <u>This is an incorrect assumption.</u>

Your interpretation of classic values (many are addressed in Trait #1, Integrity) may be somewhat different than the people you work with. Therefore, the values interpretation that adults pass on to the younger generation also may vary. For instance, an immigrant child who grew up poor overseas has certainly had different experiences than a child who grew up wealthy in America. A black child raised in America has a different view of the world than a Korean child who grew up in Japan. These children may grow up with the classic value of "Don't cheat" but the interpretation of what "cheating" is may vary.

Lamenting the "lack of values" is off base, because of these differing interpretations of the classic values. Some people steal routinely and do not think anything at all is wrong with it. If they get caught, their interpretation of the value does not change, they just know there is a law and they will serve a penalty.

It is not a generational issue, either. Adults complain about the lack of values of the younger generation, but in truth, each generation says that about the next generation. I remember reading a quote in an advice column over thirty years ago about the lack of respect by the younger generation. The quote came from Plato. There are great kids today just like there have always been great kids. Besides, who taught the kids whose values differ from yours? Adults did.

Therefore, you should proactively set the standard for ethical behavior, and not just by your example. This needs to be done as part of a <u>re-occurring</u> training program. Most likely, there will be a consensus of people who passively concur with the values you expect, but it is the active dissenters who can greatly harm your organization. Additionally, there are always those whose values can be molded to the norms of the organization. Inevitably and sadly, you will find some people who have never had anyone tell them what is right or wrong.

It is critical to overall morale to have an ethical workplace. You must teach it, not just assume it.

5. EXECUTE A VISION/GO IN A DIRECTION

This is a difficult principle to articulate. Within high performing organizations, that is those with superb leaders, is a constant striving for improvement. The goals do not have to be grand, nor do the rewards have to be great; it is simply a matter of the organizations going in a specific direction.

Many leaders believe that if you get the right structure in place, everything will just run smoothly. Their organizations, once basic procedures are in place, simply execute those procedures. However, those organizations that just perform a daily routine plunge into mediocrity. The routine becomes tedious. Tensions between employees increase. More sick time is taken. Overall performance suffers.

I have come to believe that everyone must be challenged in some way for peak performance. People want to belong to something that is important; if not worldwide important, at least important within its own sphere. They want to go somewhere and be part of a good team. Therefore, as a leader, you must present a challenge in some way.

I do not advocate change for change's sake. However, look at your department and determine how to keep going in a direction, either through refined objectives, incentives, additional training, or the like. I've come to believe that *if you do not take your organization in a direction, the organization will go in a direction of its own, downward.*

6. BE JOB-FOCUSED, NOT TIME-FOCUSED

Upon assumption of leadership, new leaders whose paycheck formerly depended upon an hourly wage, often make the mistake of remaining time-focused. Many new leaders believe that they only owe the company a standard day's work with respect to time. With rare exception, this is not true.

An organization picks its leaders based on their ability to influence others to get a job done. Sometimes it takes less time to accomplish a task, sometimes more time is required. *If you are drawing a salary, your organization expects you to get the job done, not just put in an eight-hour day.* It is a completely different paradigm. If you have multiple junior leaders under you, you can expect to spend much time either training or overseeing them, especially if they are new. You will not be receiving extra pay; it is your job.

I am not suggesting that you work 14-16-hour days, 6-7 days a week. That is unhealthy and your family will suffer along with you. However, there will be times when more than the eight- to ten-hour workday will be required. Most organizations are flexible enough to give their leaders time off when necessary as they understand not only the extra time required by leaders, but also the additional stress of leadership. Take the time off; it is important to recharge yourself.

If you lead with a job-focused attitude, promotion will be likely; that is the tangible benefit that should come later. Leaders get the job done. Within reason, they don't watch the clock.

7. TRAIN YOUR TEAM AS A TEAM

It is relatively easy to train individuals. Almost all American business training programs are geared toward individual training. Even "team building" events are usually conducted with similar ranking leaders (supervisors with supervisors, directors with directors, etc.) who do not work with each other on a daily basis. Leaders are then supposed to take nuggets of information away from these individual training and "team building" events and somehow make their departments perform well. It seldom works that way.

Military units and sports teams train as teams to reach common goals. This is so that when confronted with an urgent situation, all of the team members know each other and can react accordingly. There clearly is individual training but it is only to get to a common understanding and language of how the team will train. Can teams of warehouse workers, research scientists, or non-profit fundraisers train as a team?

It may sound like a strange concept and may require some creativity. However, at the least, a tabletop training exercise could be conducted so that team members can visualize how they would react and observe how their teammates would react in a given situation. The improved teamwork could lead to increased productivity or some sort of breakthrough. At the very least, it will show who the stronger team members are and who needs more individual training. Additionally, it would send a strong message that the organization cares about creating a good team.

An old commander of mine used to say *"Training is an investment, not an expense."* I came to believe that thought with a passion.

8. KNOW THE INTENTS/GOALS TWO LEVELS UP AND THE OPERATIONAL DETAILS TWO LEVELS DOWN

This concept is difficult to grasp for new leaders. It has some roots in military leadership, particularly during wartime, but it applies equally to any organization that has multiple levels of leadership. In large organizations, most leaders are a conduit between upper and lower levels. They must connect the dots from the higher levels to the lower levels of the organization.

You should know where your department fits into the overall organization. Although it is fine to ask your immediate boss for information and guidance, you should not solely rely on her to fill you in on the direction of the organization. Although she is there to help you, she cannot spend most of her time keeping her junior leaders up-to-date. *You must gain the ability to understand where your department fits in two levels up.* This will increase your dependability, save your boss time by not having to supervise you more than necessary, and will greatly help your Anticipatory Initiative. It will also demonstrate your sincere interest in the organization and position you as one who may be looked upon favorably for promotion.

If you encounter a boss who is reluctant to provide information or is suspicious of your information-gathering activities, then you are in a difficult position. Without overtly going around your boss (she still deserves your support), find out as much information as you can about the overall organization so that you can most effectively run your department.

(For those of you who are leading at the most junior level, that is, you have no junior leaders reporting to you, the paragraphs immediately below should imply to you to know your own department thoroughly).

Knowing operational details two levels down is important in understanding what your immediate junior leaders are doing and to ensure that your department is accomplishing what the overall organization requires of it. *Knowing the details is not the same as directly supervising two levels down.* Presumably, there is already a leader supervising that area. However, to properly inspect what you expect, you should know the appropriate details. You can even ask your junior leaders to supply you the details if you do not know them; that is perfectly acceptable. This will keep your junior leaders on their toes and will ensure they know that you are interested in what they are doing. It will also ensure that your junior leaders will be acting in accordance with the best interests of the overall organization.

Do not equate knowing details two levels down with micromanaging. You are looking to acquire knowledge, not to supervise subordinate departments. Some junior leaders may feel that keeping information to themselves will enhance their job security; in fact, the opposite is true. No one is indispensable and withholding information breeds mistrust in the work environment. If a junior leader is reluctant to share information, you need to tell that leader that sharing knowledge is not only appropriate, but necessary for maximum effectiveness and efficiency.

9. DEVELOP A SENSE OF RESPONSIBILITY IN YOUR PEOPLE

In Chapter 4, Indicators of Effective Leadership, I defined Organizational Discipline as "In the absence of the leader or key personnel, the organization executes well and initiates appropriate action." *If you have developed a sense of responsibility among your junior personnel, you are far more likely to have organizational discipline.*

Developing this sense of responsibility requires skillful planning and instilling a sense of pride in the department. Assigning small tasks to employees to build their confidence, and for you to gauge their competence, is essential. Employees should feel they have a real stake in the performance of the department and they will feel this if given tasks that affect the outcome of the department.

Even though you delegate a particular task, you do not escape responsibility for its execution. That is why you inspect what you expect. However, a much overlooked part of delegating is the training required of personnel so that they can properly accomplish the delegated task. *Never delegate a task to someone who is incapable of accomplishing that task.*

The leadership trap with this principle is "He won't do it, so I'll do it for him." If you fall into this trap, you will be cheating your other employees out of the time and energy that they deserve from you. If you get sick or go on vacation, what will happen? You must delegate and hold accountable.

There will be those who fail to complete delegated tasks satisfactorily, either through incompetence or apathy, but you should be able to identify these people quickly. Once these laggards see others develop task completion skills and increased confidence, they may see the light and want another chance. You are doing something right if this occurs.

Hopefully, your senior leaders will be doing the same for you at your level. Seek additional responsibility as appropriate. However, if you believe that additional responsibility might interfere with your primary leadership responsibilities, you need to make that fact known. Senior leaders should understand this, so do not feel as if you are inadequate. If the additional responsibility will interfere, there is usually a workaround or compromise available, so as a rule, do not turn down additional assignments. Your leader is trying to develop an increased sense of responsibility in you. Take advantage of it.

10. PRAISE IN PUBLIC, REPRIMAND IN PRIVATE

Although leaders routinely believe money is the primary motivation for workers, most surveys on employee motivation indicate that a pat on the back, a "thank you" in essence, is more prized. Money is important, of course, but recognition from the boss is more important to keeping morale up. This translates into a better work product.

If your organization is large enough, an established awards system will work wonders, even if the awards are largely a formal pat on the back. Almost everyone truly appreciates an acknowledgment in front of their fellow workers. This can become a very valuable tool, especially in an organization that has well-defined metrics or quotas.

However, it is the almost daily interaction in the workplace with a boss that an employee most appreciates. *Leaders that exhibit a knowledge of an employee's job and show appreciation that the employee is doing that job well is very powerful, if done sincerely.* Do this routinely in the workplace.

Conversely, chastising an employee in front of others can have a devastating effect not only on that particular employee, but also on those hearing the encounter, who may wonder if they are going to be next. Some leaders feel it is necessary to exhibit their authority or control in a confrontational manner, so as to say "I'm the boss." However, the level of respect accorded you depends on your actions. Public, loud confrontations are almost guaranteed to lessen respect for you, and the employee is now a malcontent who will influence others negatively. This will lead to lower morale and poorer performance.

Rather, deal with problems behind closed doors with only the minimum number of people required. *Reprimands or thorny issues are never comfortable for anyone, but they must be dealt with directly and as soon as possible.* Delaying the inevitable allows issues to fester and <u>never</u> improves a situation. If at all possible, get a positive outcome or understanding, and take the high, ethical road. Difficult employees must be dealt with firmly, but if the leader allows this sort of situation to degrade into a shouting match, the incident will become common knowledge. Loss of respect for you may be the result.

If an employee insists upon a confrontation publicly, use the level of firmness necessary to get him out of the public eye. Then, later, fill the information void by addressing the issue with other employees as necessary (see Principle #2). You may feel that "it is none of their business" but any public incident will be hanging out there with negative rumors attached unless the issue is addressed in some forum. Details need not be provided, but reassure everyone that the situation was handled professionally.

Employees deserve to be in a workplace that is positive and that reinforces good behavior. You set the tone for this. Almost everyone reacts favorably to public praise; no one reacts well to public criticism.

Chapter 8

IMPORTANT DEFINITIONS AND SOME SERIOUS LOGIC

Every leader eventually hears two sentences: "You are responsible" and "You will be held accountable." "Authority" needs to be added to this mix because without authority, it is invalid to tell leaders that they are responsible and will be held accountable.

Below are definitions for these terms along with what they mean to leaders, followed by some guidance to ensure you understand how these words interrelate.

Responsibility - That for which one must answer to his seniors or juniors

A leader is responsible for what his people do or <u>fail to do</u> as well as the physical assets and money under his control.

Authority - The legitimate power of a leader to direct those junior to him, or to take action within the scope of his position

A leader is responsible for exercising his authority to accomplish the desired outcome.

Accountability – The reckoning, when the leader answers for his actions and accepts the consequences, good or bad

Accountability is the essence of one's leadership credibility. It establishes the reasons for and the importance of leadership decisions and actions in the eyes of both seniors and juniors alike.

The Serious Logic.

Many times, junior leaders are asked about issues in which they have an interest or may have responsibility for, but over which they may have little or no control. Leaders should ask for the authority to control issues in which they have an interest.

As an example, one of my former junior supervisors was asked by my boss repeatedly about a monthly statistic that was e-mailed company-wide. The mostly inaccurate statistic was put out company-wide by an individual not in our facility, yet it reflected poorly on our facility. Although my junior supervisor was a little frustrated at the inaccuracies, he did not understand the magnitude of my boss's concern, because it also reflected poorly on him (and me for that matter).

I urged him to take control, but eventually I had to spell it out a bit more than I wanted to. I showed him a similar statistical format from another part of the company and told him to provide the statistic himself along with the raw data and any possible supporting material. He e-mailed this package monthly ahead of the individual's company-wide e-mail. His accurate data was readily accepted as the truth.

He had the interest (coming from my boss) to correct the statistic, but in his own mind, he lacked the authority. I eventually I had to "authorize" him so that he would stop getting continuous questions on his supposedly substandard performance. If he had sought the authority himself early on, his performance would never have been in question.

The truth:

- *Whoever has the interest has the responsibility*

- Responsibility without authority is difficult at best

- *If you have the interest, get the authority*

- You will be held accountable

Do not put yourself in a position of having to answer for things over which you have little or no control.

Chapter 9

IF YOU HAVE HIRING AND FIRING AAUTHORITY

You live with a bad personnel decision for a long time. Therefore, be very careful whom you hire. Too often, leaders fall into the trap of hiring someone quickly to fill a job when they should be spending more time getting the right person. When hiring, ensure that the qualifications are there and that the personality is a good fit for the culture of the organization. Otherwise, it's going to be painful. Proficiency, and eventually morale will suffer.

Let them know early on what you expect. Hopefully, this will be done before you even hire them, but if not, spell out expectations very quickly. This means that *you must know what you expect of new employees.* Generalities are not very useful in this situation; otherwise people will revert to Reality #2, "People Do What They Know."

In most large organizations, there are processes and strict requirements for terminating an employee. If the wrong person was hired to begin with, it may take a very long time before that employee is eventually terminated. Even if you do not have to go through a lengthy process, the wrong person's attitudes and actions, surely poor when he was on the job, will linger for some time after he leaves.

Be tactfully direct with problem people. When necessary, create a clear paper trail detailing the poor performance and what should be done to improve it, give him an opportunity to improve, and then do the right thing for the organization. <u>Focus on behavior, not personality</u>. It is difficult to change someone's personality and it should never be part of the work effort to do so. Behavior in the workplace, however, affects everyone and should be corrected as necessary. It is also legally defensible should the need arise.

If you must let someone go, do it quickly and directly. Long explanations should not be necessary; the employee should already know of the poor performance. Do not use anyone else's name as part of any disciplinary process; this is your decision and you must execute it. For most leaders, firing is an uncomfortable process. Have the correct facts, be direct, and anticipate the different reactions possible. Request security if necessary.

In cases involving hiring and firing, get the input of your immediate boss and of those peers whose opinions you trust. Personnel decisions are usually the most difficult, but also the most the impactful on an organization. Seek guidance.

Chapter 10

OTHER THOUGHTS

The Smartest People Listen

There is an old obscure saying that "Dumb people talk, smart people listen." Since I have advised you to communicate positively and proactively, I certainly can not now say that talking is inappropriate; however, it is true that smart people listen very well, with an innate sense of curiosity. They listen to a wide variety of viewpoints and try to understand all of them. When making decisions, it helps to understand multiple points of view. Listening well aids in this understanding.

As You Move Up, Improve; Do Not Fundamentally Change

I once knew a young employee whose supervisor wanted to make him a team leader. The young man was qualified and would have filled the role well except that his example of how a team leader should act was his previous team leader who was overly dominating, scheming, and not much fun to be around. Upon promotion, the young man started to act just like his old team leader and he quickly alienated the employees under him as well as his supervisor. He failed to realize he was being promoted because of who he was and his potential for future development; he was not being promoted to act like a domineering blowhard. Despite his supervisor's best efforts, the young man was demoted back to his old job within months.

If you are being promoted, it is because the organization believes in your character and your potential to lead. It makes no sense to become someone else. Improve your skills, watch other leaders, and learn any way you can, but do not fundamentally change who you are upon promotion.

The young man mentioned above worked his way back to the team leader position and did quite a good job by being himself.

Create Your Own Circumstances

Whenever I look back to see where I went wrong, I look to see if I <u>made</u> things happen or if I <u>let</u> things happen. When I use this prism, I almost always see where I could have influenced people or events before the actual big mistake occurred. It can be a painful recollection. Sometimes it is difficult to realize beforehand that if A happens, then the stage is set for B or C to occur. It is like putting a box on a set of stairs. Maybe nothing will happen, but the stage is certainly set for someone to get hurt. This logic applies almost everywhere. Take care of A, so that B or C do not turn into a big mistake.

You Are Going to Make Mistakes

Even if you create your own circumstances, you are going to make mistakes. It took me quite a while to figure out that I wasn't going to get fired, or worse, for making mistakes. Within reason, your boss is probably looking at how you react to the mistake more closely than the mistake itself. As long as you are competent and honest and have not put the entire organization in jeopardy, you will recover. Be calm, think the issue through, tell your boss how you are going to fix it, and then do so. However, do not make the same mistake again. That brings your learning capacity, and hence your intelligence, into question.

Bad News is Like Dead Fish

Bad things will always happen; not telling people as quickly as possible will only make things worse. Your seniors will need to know because they presumably have a wider knowledge of the enterprise and can gauge the effects on a broader basis. Your juniors need to know because rumors will begin and they can go in any direction, most of them in the wrong direction which will take even more time and energy to overcome. Gather the facts appropriate to each level and report them. Update as appropriate. The stench of bad news, like dead fish, only gets worse over time. Report it, correct it, and move on.

Other Thoughts

Diversity is about Respect

When I think of diversity, I primarily think of Reality # 7, Everybody Wants to be Treated with Respect. In large organizations, the concept of respecting people from all cultures is a normal part of the work environment; it's an expectation for anyone who wants to work there.

Hopefully, the associated programs within an organization emphasize cultural similarities and using multiple viewpoints and talents. Programs that emphasize differences and have a focus on what to say and do will be ineffective; they may actually breed resentment, not understanding and camaraderie. My travels around the world with the Marine Corps clearly showed me that people from different cultures have far more in common with each other than they have differences.

Importantly for businesses, respect for diversity is also noticed by customers. It is possible to lose business if your organization does not engender respect for all people.

Information is to be Shared

The best organizations share knowledge routinely. Too many people, including leaders, hold information too closely. When this occurs, an organization is not performing to optimal levels. With the exception of personnel information or proprietary information on products or services which would be of value to competitors, information should be shared as much as possible throughout an organization. It breeds trust, a sense of camaraderie, and a common purpose.

Learn to Plan

At some point, you are going to have to plan a project or activity. Without taking a course in Project Management, you can plan simple projects if you utilize your resources. Resources normally include people (and their brainpower), hard assets, money, and time.

Using a timeline to break out sub-elements of the plan is critical; it helps to focus everyone and gives you an idea if the project will come to fruition. Start with the completion date and work backwards to the current date. If you have other people that need to do their own planning towards your larger plan, ensure they have plenty of time to complete their work.

Get help if needed, but definitely learn how to plan. The old adage "Failing to plan is planning to fail" is true the vast majority of the time.

Writing Skills Matter

In most large organizations, writing skills are an unspoken qualifier for promotion. Employee evaluations cover mostly every area that is important to an organization, but usually, little reference is made directly to writing skills; additionally, most bosses I've seen will not talk to an employee directly about his writing skills. It seems too sensitive a subject.

The military has standard templates for Positions Papers, Information Papers, and the like, all with a different, specific purpose. I never paid too much attention to them until later in my career when they became essential to relay information succinctly. As I found out both in being a leader and in briefing more senior leaders, the higher you are in the chain, the more succinct you must be. Senior leaders in both the military and civilian world preside over an extremely wide range of areas, and they simply do not have the time to digest a long, drawn out sequence of logic.

When writing, get to the point quickly and then explain the rationale. Do not offer the rationale up front with the punch line at the end; the senior leader has lost interest by then. If your e-mails and reports can not get to the point quickly and logically, and poor spelling and grammar are evident, your credibility, and even your intelligence, will be questioned.

If you are serious about your credibility, take a writing class or get some books to help you. (I highly recommend Strunk and White's *The Elements of Style*. It is a short, easy-to-read classic text on writing). There are few bosses who will tell you your writing skills are not up to par, but they will be thinking it the next time a promotion opportunity arises.

Two People Cannot be in Charge

There is only one head coach, only one president, only one Pope. Even when equivalent employees get together to decide something, it is really their senior leader who approves or disapproves the group decision. There is a reason for this; there ultimately must be responsibility and accountability. This is not bad; it is just a fact of the leadership dynamic. Do not be fooled; only one person can make the ultimate decision for an organization. Any attempt otherwise will only lead to confusion and disarray.

Other Thoughts

Equivalent Leaders Should Help Each Other

You have probably heard the saying "It's lonely at the top." Is it? Actually, those at the top have plenty of others with whom to talk. They find equivalent leaders with whom to share experiences, to help each other improve, or maybe just to have fun.

It can and should be that way for all levels of leadership. Ideally, within your organization, there are equivalent leaders who support each other on an ongoing basis. If this is not the case, you should seek out friends or acquaintances with other organizations who are at the same, or nearly the same, level of leadership as you. Since there is, and should be, some distance between the leader and the led, being able to discuss leadership issues freely with peers is crucial to development. They are the only ones who understand your paradigm with regard to goals, processes, and personnel issues.

The equivalent leaders you choose to interact with should be trustworthy and non-judgmental. Sometimes that is difficult within an organization. There may be some jealousy or promotion competition amongst peers. In this situation, a peer may purposely offer bad advice. Those leaders who are destructive during these times will lose the respect of their peers and consequently will lose some influence within the organization. I have repeatedly told my children and many co-workers, there will always be one or two friends who will disappoint you. Ensure that the peers in your organization are trustworthy.

A truly first-rate organization encourages leadership peers to interact. A sense of camaraderie and trust develops and the organization benefits as a whole. Upon possibility of promotion, there may be some competition, but it is done with a healthy spirit, not in a destructive, negative way.

When dealing with equivalent leaders, take the high road, be a true friend, and encourage others to do the same.

When Good Employees Go Bad

Generally speaking, when a good employee starts performing poorly, it may be something <u>outside the workplace</u> that is causing his performance to suffer. Is his marriage in trouble? Does he have crushing debt? Did a parent recently die? You will learn this only if you talk to the employee. If you are respected and trusted, he should have no trouble confiding in you.

Abraham Maslow was a psychologist who studied successful people, unlike some other famous psychologists who studied less successful or mentally ill people. Maslow believed that people are basically good and that their actions could be explained by the satisfaction of a hierarchy of needs, which encompasses five levels. As one level of need is satisfied, then satisfying the next need level becomes the focus of the individual. This is called Maslow's Ladder and is condensed below.

Physiological Needs – Food, water, sleep, air

Safety Needs – A home, family, physical security

Love Needs – Belonging to a group, being accepted by others

Esteem Needs – Feeling good about a level of competence, recognition for excellence

Self Actualization – Becoming all that one is capable of becoming, maximizing potential

Without physiological needs being met, one can not move on to safety needs. One can not move on to love needs until there is a sense of security exemplified by a safe place to live and a family in some form. And so on.

If a good employee starts to perform poorly, examine why. He may have been at the esteem needs level and something has happened to move him down to the love needs or even the safety needs level.

Do not make the mistake of assuming it is not your problem. It is your problem because the quality of work expected has diminished. That happens to all of us at one time or another and it helps to have a boss who will offer good advice or who will just listen. If you can, help alleviate the problem. However, there is no magical solution for every problem when this happens; you must balance the needs of keeping a normally good employee versus the needs of the organization.

Most Meetings Should Last Less than an Hour

There are not many bigger wastes of time than meetings, unless you plan them well. Periodic informational meetings are fine as long as there is a format that is strictly followed and chatter is kept to a minimum. These types of meetings may last no more than ten to fifteen minutes or may last up to an hour. If they routinely last an hour or longer, then you want to re-examine your format or the purpose of the meeting.

Other Thoughts

For meetings to discuss a particular topic, send out preliminary information to be read prior to the actual meeting. Ensure they read it (yes, ask them beforehand if they have read it); this will focus everyone. Have an agenda that you pass out at the beginning of the meeting and stick to it. Encourage everyone to participate to get the best ideas; this will also help your future meetings as everyone will feel they have a stake in the decision-making process. However, rein in chatter that is getting off topic.

When you have the information you need, dismiss the meeting. Let whoever wants to linger to do so, but let those who must go depart the meeting at a definite ending point. After a few meetings like this, your people will become familiar with the format. You will actually get <u>more</u> input because people will know they will not be there indefinitely, and therefore will not be afraid to contribute ideas.

Sometimes there are major decisions that may require more than an hour for a meeting; however, these meetings should be the exception, not the rule.

Do not confuse these suggestions about meetings with brainstorming sessions. Brainstorming sessions should be freewheeling. The information above relates solely to informational meetings and meetings to discuss a particular topic.

<u>A Guide for Behavior</u>

My last duty in the Marines was with the U.S. European Command in Stuttgart, Germany. This is a joint command (all the services contributed personnel on a designated basis) and was the highest level of the U.S. military in Europe. Although it was a great experience with wonderful travel opportunities, we were expected to represent America well and you can imagine that our actions were constantly scrutinized. We had a particular rule for behavior. Behave as if your actions could wind up on the front page of a newspaper.

Ensure that your actions can meet that sort of scrutiny. Will your actions embarrass your family? Your organization? It is a pretty good rule for behavior.

Chapter 11

POST-MAYORAL COMMENTS

When I won my campaign in 2007 to be the forty-eighth Mayor of Indianapolis, the reactions throughout the city were interesting, to say the least. A complete unknown to much of the citizenry, most only knew I had spent 23 years as a Marine. The citizens, in true Indy fashion, were gracious and helpful. The comments by local pundits, however, ranged from hopeful to less than kind. Several mentioned that I had no experience whatsoever. That was true in the political/governing area, but it was far from true when it came to leadership.

Having led men and women in one way or another since 1978, I had already experienced many leadership challenges, both in war and peace. I had a good sense of who I was, and had been in great organizations and organizations that needed a good deal of help. There is always more to learn, but I had a good handle on the basics of how to get things done and to motivate people to success.

Having written the first edition of this book helped. Even though the book is purposely brief, it still required a tremendous amount of research. I had 23 years of military leadership and a few years of mid-level corporate leadership, but I also wanted to ensure I knew as much about the different types of leadership as possible. Teaching seminars at a local university and to a local business before my run for Mayor began created additional focus. I had a good base of knowledge.

However, the political world is different. During the campaign, I was frequently coached to say certain things, which were factual, but it was made clear to me that I didn't need to know much else about the subject. It was the press conference or political point that was important, not necessarily the substance behind the point. You can imagine that did not sit well with a 23-year Marine. It was a struggle with my small campaign staff, since I ran a shoestring campaign the first time around.

Once in office, that same expectation was present, along with others. Such as, when you go to events, only stay 15 minutes or a half hour, get your picture taken and let people know you were there, and then move on. Or that people only want to see the officeholder, not the spouse; keep her in the background. Or to hire people more for their political connections than their competence.

Post-Mayoral Comments

I did none of those things. I developed a reputation for going to events and staying, long past anyone ever expected. To me, it was about supporting the cause, not getting a photo op. I talked to so many different people by doing this; it helped me tremendously in governing the city. And because I was out almost every night, people believed I was everywhere and went to every event. It was a good reputation to have, but it was real, not manufactured.

My wife, Winnie, accompanied me whenever she could. Since we were empty nesters, I told my team that if anyone wanted me to attend an event after 5 PM or on the weekend, then they were going to get Winnie and me. That was just the way it was going to be. Soon, people started to not only notice, but also insisted that my wife come with me. It was remarkable. Within a year or so, even if I would go to a luncheon, people were asking "Where's Winnie?" Going against the conventional political wisdom and doing what I believed to be right proved to be enormously popular in the city.

In any organization, hiring people is critical, but in politics, many people expect that different rules should apply. It is true that you should hire those who are loyal and who you trust, but competence should be the baseline, not the political connection. Indianapolis has about 7000 employees, and the vast majority of them work from administration to administration, like police, fire or public works personnel. But I did hire those who worked directly for me (about 25-30 people) and had influence on hiring the next layer also. Some were connected, but all were incredibly competent. These would be the people guiding the city, so their level of competence was very important to me.

I don't ever recall asking a potential employee if he or she was a Republican or Democrat. There was a screening process before I weighed in, but even then, my team knew that competence was the baseline. We wound up hiring many Democrats, but I didn't know they were of the other party until later, because I never asked the question.

People always want a different type of elected official. They now had one. Three and half years into my first term, we did some polling and found that about 75% of the people in Indianapolis did not see me as a "politician." When writing about my eight years as the Mayor just before I left office, the local newspaper Page 1 headline was "Not a Politician."

It still amazes me the number of people who come up to me and say they appreciated that whatever I did as Mayor, it was seen as being for the city and its people, not for me or any specific organization or vested interest. That's heartwarming, but also sad in a way that people expect most elected officials to act otherwise.

All that time leading people in different settings since my early 20s made me a better Mayor. I thought it would be interesting, therefore, as an addition to the original printing of this book, for me to talk about how my Small Unit Leadership tenets held up in the political arena and having a workforce of around 7000 people.

Realities

Everybody Wants to Be on a Good Team was absolutely true on two different levels. First, citizens want to be proud of their city. Creating a buzz about the city, having a strong and improving quality of life, gaining the national spotlight in any number of ways, all made people proud of Indianapolis. I always loved Indy and spending 23 years on active duty in the Marines only increased my admiration for the people in the city. I would come home on leave about once a year to see my parents and I could see the improvement. The humble courteousness was always there, even as the city grew.

While I was the Mayor, we won the bid for the Super Bowl and then executed what is still considered the best Super Bowl week ever. I walked the Super Bowl Village as often as I could, talking to everybody and it was clear to me that many people were now seeing their city the way that I always saw it, great people capable of performing great events on a national or international stage. Many local citizens now knew what so many people from around the country already knew, that Indy is quite the city, as we like to say "No Mean City." Because of the visibility of the Super Bowl, the level of pride in the city became much higher than before and it has remained. But as I told many at the time, winning the Super Bowl bid was not a culmination of anything, it was just continuing proof that Indy was doing the right things for a long time and that it will continue.

The second way in which this Good Team reality was proven true was in attracting great people into my administration. Since I knew so few of the major figures in the city when I was first elected, I am still humbled at how many of them helped me recruit great talent. That talent clearly wanted to be on a special team that would make a difference in the city. And they did make that difference.

If you are not aware, many people love working for the government despite the lower pay, longer hours, and the headaches associated with it all. They want to make a difference. Please don't let the headlines about a few bad apples in government make you lose faith. Even if you disagree with their political philosophy, most people who work in government for a short time feel it's their duty to bring their skill set to work on behalf of the people.

I was able to draw great talent, who performed spectacularly, which then brought more good people in, because Everybody Wants to Be on a Good Team. Lots of elected officials lose great talent at the end of their first term and are not able to find equivalent talent in subsequent terms. That did not happen to me. When some people left, they were replaced with more great people and in some cases, we were able to hire game-changing, superior talent because they knew the reputation of the administration. I always joked that of those that did leave, they never really left, they just got paid by somebody else. That was because they were still willing to help even though they were working for someone else. The net effect was that the level of knowledge and talent actually got deeper and broader, something that benefited all the citizens of Indianapolis.

I never wanted to talk about my legacy (but the press always wanted to), but I did mention frequently near the end of my time as Mayor that the best thing we did was to create a new generation of leaders for the city and the region. I had an unbelievable group of individuals in their 20s and 30s who were extremely talented and were given a chance to succeed. All of them have moved on to terrific, meaningful jobs, many of them very high profile jobs such as the heads of the Chamber of Commerce and the Indiana Sports Corporation, while still young (by my standards).

People Do What They Know certainly was true. Whenever a new idea surfaced that had to be vetted, asking numerous people how they felt about the idea remained a necessity, but I had to understand from what prism they were viewing the idea. For instance, creating a new event that would draw thousands of people into a particular area summoned caution from the Public Safety people. The Public Works folks would be worried about its effect on the infrastructure. Other departments had similar parochial concerns. I had to be able to sort out whether the advice was typical, informed caution from a particular sector, or was it a true warning that the event should not go forward.

Having experienced people around you who can see the greater good is always a great idea, but they may not always be available. You need to be able stay focused on the overall objective, and then differentiate those who are giving advice from a narrower perspective from those who are coming from a more holistic perspective. Neither perspective is bad, it's just critical to know the difference.

When I think of There is Authority and Then There is Power, I can think of few situations more applicable than government. I was lucky that Indy has what is considered a "strong Mayor" framework. Most of the city government is actually run by the Mayor. Most people don't know that, throughout the country, there are widely varying authority models of local governments. Some mayors are essentially the senior city councilor. Others are figureheads, with the city actually run by a city manager or a board. There are variations on all of these frameworks all across the nation. In almost all cases, the perceived power of the Mayor usually exceeds the actual authority.

This makes sense. Since leadership is about influence, electing someone with the title of Mayor means something; it sends a signal throughout the community. Certainly, in major cities across the nation, no one wants to be on the wrong side of the Mayor. I was far from arrogant, and I developed a reputation for not retaliating politically (something which is unfortunately quite common in government), but still people wanted to know where the Mayor stood on almost everything. Other government agencies, businesses, nonprofits, and others look to the Mayor and the administration for a signal. One obvious example is with foundations that are in the business of donating money to good causes. If the city used some of its discretionary money, such as arts funding, on particular organizations, then that would be interpreted as that organization had been vetted and was doing good work. Money from other sources would then feel more comfortable to donate.

This is a powerful tool, particularly when used with commercial business, and as such would need to be cautiously used. But there is no doubt it is there.

Indy has had a string of well-respected mayors going back to the 1960s, because we all worked well with the business community and the nonprofit sector. That said, they wanted to work with the Mayor and the administration, all pulling in the same direction.

This reality about authority and power can work in reverse. I have seen a legislative body ignore a government official in an executive position because he had squandered his influence. Instead of working with the executive, as should be the case, they passed legislation as they saw fit, which then put the executive in awkward circumstances. It wasn't pretty. Once a leader loses the power that comes with legal authority, his days are numbered.

Of all of the Leadership Realities pertaining to political life, none could be more understated than Even Good Change Creates Friction. It takes only very little observation to see that representatives of Party A can oppose ideas presented by Party B, yet if the exact same idea is presented by a member of Party A, then all those Party A representatives will follow that same idea blindly. It's really quite a sight to behold. Both Democrats and Republicans are guilty of this and it is unbelievably easy to see.

If an elected official actually wants to do the right thing for the community, it is very difficult to work through this dynamic. I can't tell you the number of times that a member of my administration or I was quietly told by people that an idea is a good one, but they have to come out publicly against us because of the difference in parties. And the spin doctors, who are numerous and easy to find, (and unfortunately necessary) are very anxious to ply their trade, which is good for the media because conflict in politics keeps people watching. It's a weird, frequently counterproductive system.

Special interests, jockeying for the next election, the internal dynamics in a party caucus, and many other factors come into play. Because of the great talent in my administration, we accomplished almost everything we wanted to; however, near the end of my second and final term, politics won out on a couple of issues and the people of Indianapolis lost as a result. Anybody who was truly following those issues knew that the opposition "was for it before they were against it."

This is where it's important to know who you are. A former great governor of Indiana, Mitch Daniels, once said something that sticks with me to this day. When referring to politicians, he said "Some people want to be something, others want to do something." Far too many politicians want to be something. We should elect those who want to do something, and are willing to be courageous in the attempt.

Your Way is Not the Only Way should be standard for elected officials, particularly those in an executive position. If you have a strong staff, as I did, you should want as many ideas coming forward as possible. You should vet every idea, but the origin of the idea should be irrelevant.

One of the odd parts of politics is that the elected official will not only get the credit for a good idea, but the person whose idea it was, wants the elected official to get the credit. It's just the way it works. Very often, I would attempt to give credit where it was due, but the staff largely discouraged me from doing so. The feeling is, it's all about the officeholder, who they want to get re-elected. I frequently won these mini-battles and praised my staff publicly. However, in the eyes of the press and the citizens, I still got the credit. It was very uncomfortable at times for a Marine.

For far too many elected officials, micromanaging is the norm and every idea has to come from the top. It's clear paranoia, very common in politics, and at times funny to watch, but it's the citizens who matter and frequently much less is getting done than should get done. Sometimes, great ideas don't even get discussed.

In the political arena, In the Absence of Affirmative Leadership, Someone Else Will Fill the Void is applied differently but is still relevant.

First, an elected officeholder finds out quickly that to get an issue out in front of the public means getting out there first, usually through the media. If there are contentious issues, the first side out with the story drives the narrative and usually wins the argument in the eyes of the public. The opposition has to catch up and try to portray a different side. It's very difficult to do and requires so much more time, energy, and resources.

I was late to the game on this. I just wanted to work on policy and early on, I left the media to the experts to speak on my behalf. They were good at it, but they also knew that people wanted to hear from the elected official, not a spokesperson. They tried to tell me this, but I wasn't listening very well in the beginning. It was playing catch up all the time that made me see the light. After a while, I learned the rhythms of the media and my staff would try to anticipate the opposition's moves so that we could be first. This sounds so political, but getting out first publicly actually saved so much time and energy that could be used on actual policy, that it was worth it.

The second way this reality is relevant, I have briefly discussed above. If an elected executive loses his influence, he can expect the legislative body to start driving the action. The public wants their elected executives to be exceedingly competent, but if the perception is otherwise, then there will be some dysfunction. There will usually be an attempt by some staff to make the executive seem in command, but those in the circle will know otherwise. A wise observer will be able to see the difference.

Traits

Integrity - This is a trait that everyone wishes elected officials had in common. I do believe that most people get into politics to do good, to make a difference. However, I always told my children that some of their best friends will let them down, and that is how I feel about the issue of integrity and elected officials. Some officials just get lost along the way, and we read about them far too frequently. There are egregious violations and some people just can't stay clear of the corruption.

There are elected officials who don't go to work most days. Many officials can get away with this because they hire people to run the office day-to-day and the citizens don't notice anything wrong at all. This is more common than most people know. And it's legal.

I also sadly know of another official who gave it all away for a $5000 bribe. He embarrassed his family and spent time in jail. He was basically a good man who lost his way. That is why knowing who you are is truly important. It helps keep you on the right path.

The rules are frequently murky and sometimes what is a well-meaning gesture toward someone could actually be a violation when it comes to politics. That is why it is important for those new to politics to ensure they have knowledgeable and loyal people who can keep them on the correct path. Having what I affectionately call "political hacks" around me was important; they know the rules in detail, have a historical knowledge, and can anticipate how certain actions will be perceived, legal or otherwise. They are actually important to the process.

Competence - This is hit and miss when it comes to elected officials. Most people elected to a position for the first time could not possibly know everything about that job. Citizens are counting on the official to be intelligent, able to learn quickly, and then act in accordance with the needs of the citizenry with the power inherent in the office. You are essentially trusting their judgment when you elect them. I have found that executive government positions are filled by men and women who are generally competent, because neither party wants high profile positions filled by someone who would embarrass them. You may disagree with their policies, but they are, for the most part, intelligent and competent.

Some lower level legislators and lower government positions are a different story. There are many who are rewarded for their loyal work to the party; essentially political workers who have been "promoted." Some are very competent and work hard; however, there are too many who have been rewarded for their loyalty but really have no place being in office.

Energy – If you're doing it right, holding elected office requires a vast amount of energy, both mental and physical. This means staying in shape and getting the proper amount of rest. The people deserve this. Some may not want to be as active as I was, but a certain level of energy is required, especially in high-pressure positions, such as Mayor or Governor.

I was very open about why I did not run for a third term; I did not feel that I could give the same amount of energy as I did the previous eight years. I worked hard and was at as many events as possible, and that took a toll. I simply did not think it was fair to the citizens of Indianapolis if I could not maintain the same pace.

Decisiveness – Too many people in office are wishy-washy on their beliefs. They don't want to offend anyone or they want to poll a particular issue for cover. If they are in a gerrymandered area, they can decide on nothing indefinitely. That may be OK on some minor issues, but on major issues, elected officials should take a principled stand, and let it be known. The people deserve this and appreciate this.

The military helped me greatly in this regard. Gather the facts and make a decision. I learned in the military that if you are 70-80% there, then trust your gut and go. I pretty much did this as the Mayor. Elected officials should have a bias for action. I certainly did and even if some disagreed and weren't sure why we were doing something, they trusted that we were acting on principle. They at least knew we were doing it for the right reasons, for something that we believed would help the city.

Loyalty – This is absolutely critical in political life. As I've said above, an elected official needs competent people around him, but they also must be loyal. During our initial transition into office, we tried to maintain some people from the previous administration for continuity. However, we found out rather quickly that some of them were utterly disloyal and hurt our efforts to better the city. What I said above about spending much more time to unwind or defend a story than to initiate a story applies. Thankfully, we found out within months who they were and we asked them to move on.

A newly elected official must be very careful in who he or she trusts. After I won my first election (a big upset), dozens upon dozens of people came out of the woodwork to "help." Some were legitimate, some were not. Thankfully, I had enough people around me who I trusted that knew how to sort them out. Sorting out those who want to and can help from those who just want to be seen with you is a crucial skill to learn.

Lots of people just want to hang around the elected official to make themselves look better, to create an illusion of closeness to the official, or sometimes just hoping to get some perks. I even seemed to have more "cousins" than I did before the election. Every few weeks, someone would come to me and say they had met my "cousin," usually someone I had never heard of before. Loyal people are needed to help with this phenomenon.

As I've said before, I was very lucky to have had a great staff and friends who are still very loyal.

Anticipatory Initiative – I would say routinely that the basics of the Mayor's job is to get the fundamentals right (like infrastructure, public safety, etc.), which are hard, but also to anticipate the future and beat every other city there. A Mayor must create a city that attracts talent and therefore businesses. This means understanding trends, knowing what citizens want (which can change by generation), and positioning your city appropriately. You must create the city that people want to live in. This requires an enormous amount of Anticipatory Initiative from a lot of people. I believe we understood this trait very well, and the growing population and business community reflected that fact.

Principles

Communicate Positively and Proactively – I can't think of a profession where this principle applies more than the political arena. That is why there are so many practitioners who specialize in political messaging. Some are great at it, especially those who can anticipate the reaction of the public or specific groups to a particular message.

The timing of communication is absolutely critical in politics. On any subject, getting your view out first is critical. If you can drive the message home with multiple communication opportunities, even better. That is because of the nature of the media today. Most local media, including Indianapolis, is even-handed and fair. However, because of shrinking margins and digital media, the experienced reporter who is balanced and has a sense of history, is rarer these days. Even worse, the young reporters are generally looking for a quick, big hit, which means trying to take down a politician or company. They want the award. The shading of the truth is obvious, but worse, young reporters, who are now the majority, do not either have the time or will to actually develop a story. They are "surface warriors," meaning whoever gets to them first gets their story into the public arena; there's no in-depth research. Therefore, those of the opposite view have to play catch up.

In some offices, such as Governor or Mayor, there is an amazing breadth of subjects on which effective communication is mandatory. I always told people that every hour of my schedule was about a different area that was important to the city. Being able to communicate in all of these areas requires one to have great people who know the areas technically but also know how to effectively message the area.

Inspect What You Expect – This is still my most difficult principle to execute. As mentioned above, there is an incredibly broad range of topics to not only understand but also to ensure that things are getting done appropriately. At a lower level of politics, one can still personally inspect what is expected, but at a much higher level, you will have to rely on your senior staff to do much of this inspecting.

Develop a Sense of Responsibility in Your People – It is important to tell your senior staff what you expect. In my case and with my background (including staff positions in the Marines), I wanted them to know that everything we did was going to be for the people and for the long term future of the city. Politics was to be secondary to any policy considerations.

I'd like to think that would be the consideration for any elected official, but it's not. For too many, the desire to stay in office trumps everything. That can lead to decisions based on getting more votes in the next election rather than what one believes is truly best for everyone.

I don't know how many times I asked a member of my staff, "What's the right thing to do?" Repeated often enough, everyone picks up on it. I also don't know how many times I heard later in my administration how much my staff appreciated that sentiment. Some had been staff of previous elected officials and that sentiment apparently wasn't uppermost in everyone's minds.

Praise in Public, Reprimand in Private – I often and routinely tried to praise my staff for their work, but it became quite clear that everything that happened while you're in office, good or bad, is attributed to you. This disturbed me because most of the success of my administration was directly attributable to a great staff. As I have mentioned, I continued to praise my staff until the end but I also knew the public perception was something different.

I can't ever recall reprimanding my staff publicly. There are occasions where you must publicly disagree with other people. That's just part of the job. If you're standing up for the city, this is required at times. However, I do remember a specific instance of a legislator convicted of corruption and a few members of my team wanted me to publish a statement condemning his actions. Politically, it could make me look like I had great integrity, but I didn't need anyone to tell me or my staff that fact. He was being roundly criticized publicly already, and I declined to pile on. A statement coming from the government executive carries even more publicity and I knew that he had young children in local schools. The last thing they needed to see was a statement from the Mayor in the paper or on TV decrying their father. There had to be enough pain going on already in that family. I never regretted that decision.

Other Thoughts

The Smartest People Listen – I'm not sure there is a profession more in need of this thought than political officeholders. So many assume offices where they may know some of the areas that apply, but, as I've said above, there is frequently a very steep learning curve for many officeholders. For instance, any Governor or Mayor of a large city covers hundreds of areas during a term. There is no possible way anyone could know the entire range of ideas when taking office. Also, many officeholders run for an office they know nothing about and have to rely completely on the professionals to get them up to speed once in office.

What citizens are counting on is the basic intelligence and hopefully curiosity of the officeholder to learn a new position very quickly and then guide it appropriately for the benefit of those citizens. This requires lots of listening.

Create Your Own Circumstances – There are so many ways to do this in the political arena. Building good will, listening to the citizens, and having good relationships with stakeholders all are important. Sometimes I did this well, other times not so much. However, I always had a good staff who was expert in this area. Setting the table, shaping the battlefield (for you military types), or whatever you call it, this always helped in advancing policy goals and in creating a favorable image in the media.

Whenever we were to make a major announcement, we privately told many people. This was to ensure that they were ready to comment favorably instead of acting surprised. Also, by shaping policies toward what the citizens generally wanted, we were able to create much goodwill. Treating everyone well and being kind and honest with them usually helped. We were certainly kind to everyone initially, but you had to earn keeping that designation with us.

You Are Going to Make Mistakes – This applies at all levels. Unfortunately, when an elected official makes a mistake, it usually finds its way into the press. It's how you react that matters. If you're new to the office, it's more painful. Some will pile on and create an impression that you're not up to the job. However, if you've built up some goodwill from your time in the office, it's easier. People are more forgiving. Either way, admit it and move on.

Bad News is Like Dead Fish – It is almost impossible to keep anything secret in the government. With the Freedom of Information Act, almost everything will eventually be available to the public, as it should be. So ensure that the staff brings the bad news to the forefront as soon as possible. Learning about a bad situation from the press is horrible, and you will never get in front of it and turn opinion, no matter what the facts are.

Equivalent Leaders Should Help Each Other – Creating this atmosphere in your staff is extremely beneficial as most areas of progress come from an interdisciplinary approach. They must understand each other and respect each other. Giving them great autonomy in a political office is unusual, but I did. It paid off. My staff was incredible because they were smart, worked together and kept the needs of the citizens in the forefront.

Most Meetings Should Last Less Than an Hour – With rare exceptions, this remains true at every level.

People are nervous at the beginning of any administration. I held a staff meeting every Monday at 9 AM. The first staff meeting, it was easy to tell that people were trying to feel each other out but the meeting went well and lasted about an hour. The second week, the meeting had gone an hour and there were still two people left to talk. I abruptly left and said this meeting should be less than an hour.

That is very unusual behavior for a Mayor, particularly for one new to the political process. However, the staff got the hint and we never had a meeting last more than an hour again. By the end of the second term, the meetings were less than half an hour. What proved to be more valuable was the staff spending the remaining time during that hour talking to each other without me being in the room. That turned into great team building time and I believe was a big part of our success.

A Guide for Behavior – Knowing that anything that I did, in public or private, could be on the front page of a newspaper was extremely beneficial to me. I'm not sure I could have given myself better advice than writing this thought years before I considered running for Mayor. This thought proved especially true during a campaign for office when people filmed me constantly at every appearance, hoping to catch a moment that would embarrass me. Combined with the proliferation of social media, particularly mean-spirited, untruthful blogs, an elected official must ensure that any actions outside of the home are above reproach.

To demonstrate how far this has gone, I was once going to go to a Halloween event dressed as a devil. My political people talked me out of it saying the picture would be used against me in the next election. That's where we are today.

Final Thought

It was both enlightening and heartwarming to compare the concepts that I believe are important to new and middle level leaders with those of executive leadership. There are many similarities, which should give hope to those who desire to rise through the ranks. In most cases, one can move up and succeed by being competent in the discipline of leadership.

The main exception would be the enormous responsibility and pressure of a chief executive who must ensure the viability and continuity of an entire enterprise. Being responsible for the well-being of a large enterprise and all of the people who have a stake in its survival and success weighs heavily on any individual. Few seek such responsibility and pressure; even fewer do it well. However, like most leadership concepts, I believe it can be learned.

Best wishes for a successful leadership journey.

APPENDIX

A SUMMARY OF IMPORTANT POINTS

Below are the key points in the body of this book. Use these as a quick refresher when needed.

Introduction

Leadership is underrated, not overrated.

Leadership is a learned behavior.

Great leadership routinely occurs at the "rubber meets the road" level.

Chapter 1

Leaders are not judged directly on how they perform, but on how those people assigned to them perform.

Chapter 2

Leadership is the ability to successfully influence a group of people to achieve a desired outcome.

Influence is the essence of what leaders do.

The desired outcome is why the leader was chosen for a particular position or responsibility.

If most of your employees are acting one way, either well or poorly, it is a direct result of your leadership.

If things are not going well, there is still leadership in your department. Either you are a bad leader or someone else is filling the leadership role in a negative manner.

People want to succeed and they want the designated leader to take them to that success.

Chapter 3

Leaders are placed in positions of responsibility to get the job done.

Leaders must look out for the welfare of their people.

These two overarching responsibilities always work together.

Chapter 4

Proficiency, Organizational Discipline, and High Morale must all must be present to indicate truly effective leadership.

No individual is properly trained until his actions contribute positively to the group.

Organizational discipline can occur only if the leader has clearly set proper standards and expectations.

High morale by itself will not allow an organization to attain its goals.

Chapter 5

No one shows up on the first day and says "I think I'll be the worst employee I can be." It just doesn't happen.

Good people want to be around other good people.

If you do not create the proper work environment, then your good, talented people will leave as soon as another opportunity presents itself.

People do what they know; if necessary, change what they know.

To effect proper change, it is least effective to just order new methods or procedures. It is most effective to bring all stakeholders into the discussion in order to explain why the change is necessary, why it will be beneficial, and to get valuable input.

Good leaders use their influence to set, change, and enforce standards.

Standards need to be realistic, enforceable, and in line with higher level organizational standards and goals.

Assume that the "power" is acting in accordance with the best intentions of the organization.

The junior must adjust to the senior.

Change will come whether we want it to or not.

Friction will occur no matter how well-planned or explained the change is.

Leaders should be visible and approachable immediately upon the implementation of any change in the work environment; this will be a calming influence.

Every employee, from the CEO to the newest temporary worker, wants to be treated with respect.

You cannot talk to higher management one way and lower level employees another way. The hypocrisy is, or will be, easily visible and will make you unworthy of respect by all levels in the organization.

Good leaders use their authority to implement ideas, no matter the source.

If you are not aware of the overall money picture and how you fit into it, you may be looked upon as naïve or "out of the loop" at the least. Senior leaders may assume you do not have the skills to understand. None of these scenarios are favorable to you.

People want to be led.

Without exception, when an authorized leader fails to exercise affirmative leadership, someone else will fill the void.

Chapter 6

Leaders are and should be held to a higher standard of integrity.

Integrity must be part of the person; it can not be a workplace habit.

The level of respect accorded you is based on more than just your position.

Leadership competence is different than technical competence.

If you have been leading people without learning about leadership from other sources besides your own experience, then you are most likely underperforming as a leader and cheating your organization and your employees out of your best effort.

All of the organizations involved, higher, lower, and adjacent, are expecting your department to do its job and do it well.

When given a task, get it done on time while exceeding expectations.

A successful leader has a level of energy about him that comes through no matter his personality.

People expect to be led by optimists.

Decisiveness is a time-saver, particularly for your employees.

Every leader should be able to talk directly and on point to juniors, seniors, and peers.

A leader's presence must be felt.

Do not show disrespect to senior leaders in front of your people.

To be an effective leader, you must be loyal up and down the chain.

Outstanding leaders anticipate required actions, usually before anyone else even knows an action may be required.

Chapter 7

To lead others effectively, you must first know yourself.

Reflective thought, mentally putting yourself in difficult situations and imagining how you would react, will help fill the experience gap.

Actively provide your people as much information as they can handle before issues arise or fester.

Be very clear in your expectations.

Checking up on what you expect is a very critical and necessary part of task accomplishment. Just because you tell someone to do something does not mean it is going to get done.

You must actively communicate the expected ethical behavior.

If you do not take your organization in a direction, the organization will go in a direction of its own, downward.

If you are drawing a salary, your organization expects you to get the job done, not just put in an eight-hour day.

Training is an investment, not an expense.

You must gain the ability to understand where your department fits in two levels up.

Knowing the details is not the same as directly supervising two levels down.

If you have developed a sense of responsibility among your junior personnel, you are far more likely to have organizational discipline.

Never delegate a task to someone who is incapable of accomplishing that task.

Leaders that exhibit a knowledge of an employee's job and show appreciation that the employee is doing that job well is very powerful, if done sincerely.

Reprimands or thorny issues are never comfortable for anyone, but they must be dealt with directly and as soon as possible.

Chapter 8

A leader is responsible for what his people do or fail to do as well as the physical assets and money under his control.

A leader is responsible for exercising his authority to accomplish the desired outcome.

Accountability is the essence of one's leadership credibility. It establishes the reasons for and the importance of leadership decisions and actions in the eyes of both seniors and juniors alike.

Whoever has the interest has the responsibility.

If you have the interest, get the authority.

Do not put yourself in a position of having to answer for things over which you have little or no control.

Chapter 9

You live with a bad personnel decision for a long time.

You must know what you expect of new employees.

In cases involving hiring and firing, get the input of your immediate boss and of those peers whose opinions you trust.

Chapter 10

The smartest people listen.

As you move up, improve; do not fundamentally change.

Create your own circumstances.

You are going to make mistakes.

Bad news is like dead fish.

Diversity is about respect.

Information is to be shared.

Learn to plan.

Writing skills matter.

Two people cannot be in charge.

Equivalent leaders should help each other.

When a good employee goes bad, the cause may be outside of the workplace.

Most meetings should last less than an hour.

A good guide for behavior is to do nothing that would embarrass your family or organization if your actions were made public.

RECOMMENDED READING

I've already recommended *Who Moved My Cheese?* by Spencer Johnson, and Strunk and White's *The Elements of Style*. I also recommend almost anything by John C. Maxwell or Perry Smith. Dr. Maxwell's *The 21 Irrefutable Laws of Leadership* is a great resource, as is Perry Smith's (Major General, U.S. Air Force, Retired) *Rules & Tools for Leaders*.

Rudy Guiliani has published an excellent book called *Leadership* and W. Edwards Deming has quite a prolific collection of books on business management. Colin Powell also has some great leadership material available. Lastly, Robert Greenleaf, who died in 1990, published several books and essays on Servant Leadership; his organization lives on and its website is www.greenleaf.org.

NOTE

Greg Ballard has written Small Unit Leadership in order to help new, junior, and middle level leaders understand their duties and improve their skills. He believes there are many potentially great leaders who were never taught leadership skills early on and consequently failed in their first attempt at leadership, never to lead again. His website is smallunitleader.com (a Facebook page) and his Twitter account is @smunitleader.

Made in the USA
Middletown, DE
24 July 2019